The 4th & final SECRET DIARY OF JOHN MAJOR

Published in Great Britain
by Private Eye Productions Ltd
6 Carlisle Street, London W1V 5RG
in association with Corgi Books

© 1995 Pressdram Ltd
ISBN 0 552 14405 3

Designed by Bridget Tisdall
Printed in England by
Ebenezer Baylis & Son Ltd, Worcester

Corgi Books are published by Transworld Publishers Ltd
61–63 Uxbridge Road, Ealing, London W5 5SA
in Australia by Transworld Publishers (Australia) Pty, Ltd
15–23 Helles Avenue, Moorebank, NSW 2170
and in New Zealand by Transworld Publishers (N.Z.) Ltd
3 William Pickering Drive, Albany, Auckland

2 4 6 8 10 9 7 5 3 1

The 4th & final SECRET DIARY OF JOHN MAJOR

Illustrated by
Caroline Holden

PRIVATE EYE · CORGI

September 1994

Monday

I have taken a not considerably major decision. I have decided that my wife Norman and I should cut short our holiday in Algarvia, to be present at one of the greatest triumphs of modern times — i.e., England's historic victory in the test match over the South Africans. It was brilliant. We made 302 for 6, I think, in reply to their 175 and then we had 204 to win. And we got it! I arrived on the balcony just in time for the finish and everyone cheered. It reminded me of the famous match at school when we played Selhurst Grammar, and I got 8 not out. What's more, my brother Terry didn't even bat. But you won't find any mention of that in his book, oh no.

Tuesday

It was just as well I came back from my holiday as today there was another historic triumph over the IRA. They have surrendered at last, in return for the British leaving Ireland. A number of people are saying that I must have made a secret agreement with them. I would like to state categorically that is totally untrue. It was Mr Mayhew who did the secret deal, while I was on holiday.

Wednesday

Someone called Mr Hanley keeps coming into my office and asking what he should do. I was in no small measure puzzled by this, until he reminded me how we had met by chance in the House of Commons canteen just before my historic reshuffle, and that I had asked him to be Party Chairman. I couldn't remember why, but then he pulled out of his wallet a photo of his mother, whom he said was a film star who was in *Genevieve*. Terry and I went to see it at the Purley Odeon when it came out, although I did not cry at the end, as Terry claims in his so-called book. The one

I cried in was *Lassie Come Home*, and I was much younger then. Terry didn't even see that one.

I told Mr Hanley that his job was to keep me away from things which make me unpopular. I was therefore very annoyed to hear him later on the News attacking my friend Jeffrey Archer over some business about share-dealing. "He should clear the air," said Mr Hanley, implying that there was some air to be cleared, which there is not, as Jeffrey has several times rung me himself to say that his hands were clean. If Mr Hanley is going to spend his time criticising loyal Conservatives, he will have to go back to the canteen and stop sitting outside my office reading the *Spectator* upside down, which he was doing when I came in this morning. I was very relieved this evening when Jeffrey sent me a fax to say that he had been found officially innocent, by his wife.

Thursday

We were woken up early this morning by a very loud noise of a man shouting in the street outside that I had "kissed the Pope's bum". I explained to my wife Norman that it was probably one of the poor mental patients whom Mrs Bottomley has let out into the community so that they can murder people. But Norman then recognised him from the television. "It is Mr Paisley, the Irish clergyman," she said.

Normally I would have asked the policeman at the door to send him away, but then I remembered that I needed Mr Paisley's votes in case there was another backbench revolt by the bastards, whose names I still have in my Bastard Book (beginning with Sir Richard Body). So I invited Mr Paisley to come and shout at me in my office. "This is a black day for the people of Northern Ireland!" he bellowed. "How dare the IRA lay down their arms. Things have come to a pretty pass when we have peace in Ulster."

Friday

Mr Portaloo is up to his old tricks, even though I humiliated him by promoting him in my reshuffle. In an effort to win popularity, he has announced his plan to beat the rail strike by making all strikes illegal in essential industries. When I called him round to explain himself, I pointed out that his plan would not include the trains, because they are not essential. "Haven't you noticed that these days everyone goes by car?" I said. He went red and stormed out, knocking over Mr Hanley who was coming in yet again to complain that the *Telegraph* crossword was awfully hard at the moment due to the fact that they had a new compiler.

Saturday

Let there be no doubt as to who is the man of the moment. "Gerry Adams," said Norman. "No, it is me," I told her as we watched the news of the ceasefire over our TV supper of Vegetarian Moussaka.

After 300 years, according to Mrs Hogg, it is me and me alone who has solved the Irish Question. Unfortunately not everyone agrees with Mrs Hogg, and troublemakers like my former friend Norma Lamont say I have "sold out to the terrorists".

As I told Mr Hanley to tell the media: "This is untrue. There is no sell-out. If you sell something you get something in return, which we clearly haven't."
People are very stupid sometimes.

Sunday

I am absolutely livid, according to the newspapers, at the decision to transfer some IRA prisoners back to Northern Ireland.

"Why was I not

told?" I said, apparently.

So I decided to ask Mr Howard why I was not told. Unfortunately he was still on holiday in a place called Colombia. So I still do not know the answer to why I am so furious.

But, make no mistake, I am a lot more furious than Mrs Thatcher would have been if it was her.

Mr Tebbit is also furious because these prisoners were the IRA bombers who tried to blow him up. Honestly, some people are so self-centred. They lack the wider vision that leads to solving world problems like I do. No one will ever call Mr Tebbit the man of the moment! Oh no.

Sunday

The ceasefire is working, and there have only been two bombs and one shooting in the last 48 hours.

Meanwhile, to show that I have not given in to the terrorists, I am continuing to refuse broadcasters permission to use Mr Adams's real voice. If people could actually hear him they might be persuaded to believe what he says. Like I did.

This refusal will really show Mr Adams who is the man of the moment.

And it won't be him.

Monday

Today I am in a place called Leyden which is in Holland, although my press adviser Mr Meyer said it was in the Netherlands. Why am I surrounded by these incompetents? People like Mr Hanley, who cannot even hold the *Spectator* the right way up when he is pretending to read it. But more of him later. Oh yes. I was in Leyden to make a very historic speech setting out my new vision of Europe. I had to do this because Mr Herr Kohl and his friend Mr Monsieur Mitterrand have been plotting to make a two-track Europe, with

some people, i.e. them, going fast in the fast lane, and other people, such as us, going slow in the slow lane. To my mind, this is quite wrong. What we need, as I made quite clear in my historic speech to the Dulverton Conservatives during the Euro-elections, is a multi-speed, multi-layered, multi-track 27-lane superhighway, with everyone free to go at different speeds

in different directions, with opt-out flyovers built-in, so that people can exit and re-enter whenever they want. This is the only way forward, or backward, or even sideways, according to which lane you are driving in. "I suppose," said my wife Norman after the speech, "Britain will be on the hard shoulder, broken down, surrounded by your famous cones." Once again, she has got the wrong end of the stick. "You do not have cones on the hard shoulder," I told her, "they are only for use on the highway itself in order to speed up traffic. It is all explained on our Cone Hotline, or there is now a new pamphlet called *The Highway Cone*, which was written by Mr Waldegrave before he was promoted in my recent reshuffle."

Tuesday

Today I made another historic speech, this time on the problem of crime. I even invented a new phrase, which Norman read out to me from the *Daily Mail*, i.e. "yob culture", which describes what has gone wrong with Britain in the last 15 years. I said that we were all sick and tired of these yobs, roaming about behaving like yobs, and that something should be done about it. What is needed, I told them, is a new partnership to deal with this problem, between us and the yobs. This would be like our partnership with Mr Adams in Ulster, which has been so successful. I am sure that we shall soon be reading headlines about all the yobs agreeing to a permanent cessation of their yobbish activities.

Just after I had written this I turned on the television and there were lots of people hitting each other with chairs at a boxing match. Fortunately Mr Hanley came on to say that it was all perfectly all right. The people fighting were just being exuberant and were not really yobs. Perhaps Mr Hanley is not so bad after all, as he has obviously drawn a very firm line under this one and we shall not hear of it again.

Wednesday

What an idiot Mr Hanley is! It was a great mistake for him to have accepted the job as party chairman when I offered it to him in the canteen. He has gone on television again to say that he was totally incompetent and that the people fighting *were* yobs after all. I called him in from the corridor, where he was trying to do the *Daily Telegraph* quick crossword, and gave him one of my famous rockets, like the one I gave Mr Paisley last week when he told me to get out of my own office (which I did — that showed him who was boss, oh yes). Anyway I asked Mr Hanley what would happen if, every time one of the government said something silly on television, we apologised for it. We'd be on TV all day long and all night, and there'd be no time for us to run the country. He laughed, which was in no way an appropriate response to my very serious point, and then asked me if I wanted his mother's autograph. He said she would do one for Terry as well, as she had really enjoyed his book and would like to meet him one day. Talking of Terry's book, which I never do, I spotted another very serious mistake on page 59. He claims that all the gnomes made by father's garden ornament business had red hats. This is totally untrue. The ones sitting on toadstools, which were a very popular line before the war, had green hats. I know this because I kept one for a long time in my bedroom, as a bookstop for my old Wisdens. I called him Cyril, after my great hero Cyril Washbrook (not to be confused with our pet squirrel Cyril, who Terry also made a mistake about, because he was really called Robert). If Terry was Mr Hanley he would go on television and apologise for all these mistakes.

Thursday

I am very considerably annoyed with Mr Reynolds, who is the prime minister of Ireland. Though not of all Ireland, oh no. I am the prime minister of some of it. He is saying that I am not moving fast enough in the peace process — i.e. removing all the troops from Ireland and recognising Mr Adams as the potential leader of his people. I will have to explain to him that I believe in a two-track peace process for Ireland. Mr Reynolds may not appreciate that although I am driving in the fast lane, I have to go slowly because I am stuck behind a very large vehicle which will not move, however much I flash my lights. Obviously in Ireland they do not have proper motorways and probably do not even have cones. No wonder Mr Reynolds is so confused.

Friday

Mr Hanley is back in my good books. He has really ticked off Mr Clarke for putting up interest rates. He said that if Mr Clarke did this again, he would have to go. This is the sort of firm, decisive leadership which we have been lacking. I bet Mr Blair wishes he had someone like Mr Hanley in his party.

Saturday

The "Hanley effect" is working! This morning he brought in the paper showing that my popularity has shot up to a record 21 percent. I am only 29 points behind Mr Blair now. By my reckoning I am now in the fast lane to victory at the next election, oh yes.

October

Monday

This week I am to be a world statesman, in time for the party conferences. This is a brilliant idea by Mr Meyer, who told me that I should start by meeting someone who is really popular so that people will think he is my friend. "How about Tony Blair?" said Mr Hanley, looking up from his *Telegraph* crossword, which incidentally was still blank after two hours.

Mr Meyer ignored him, and said that he had arranged for me to have a photo-opportunity with Mr Mandela in South Africa. This will be in no small measure a very historic meeting, since I will be the first British Prime Minister to visit

South Africa for 30 years, i.e. Mrs Thatcher was never invited to go there. Oh no.

Tuesday

Today I arrived in South Africa, which is very hot and where their national game is cricket. My wife Norman has packed my cricket bat and pads and my grey flannels, just in case I have time for a game. Which I did! I managed to bowl out their Sports Minister and luckily the television cameras caught the great moment when he knocked down the wicket with his bat and said "Well done, Prime Minister." Mr Mandela could not play cricket, because he is too old, but he very kindly allowed me to speak to his parliament which is all black, except for quite a lot of whites. This shows how tolerant they are, and they even allow their former Prime Minister to be in the Cabinet although his party lost the election by a landslide. "I hope your Mr Blair allows you this privilege when the time comes," said Mr Mandela. I had no idea what he meant, but he spent a long time in prison and is obviously completely out of touch.

Wednesday.

Mr Meyer was in high spirits this morning. "Your South African trip has made the front pages," he said, holding up a pile of newspapers. I was somewhat annoyed to see that they all had a picture of Mrs Thatcher in India with the headline "Major Fury As Thatcher Speech Ruins His SA Trip". "What is the meaning of this?" I said to Mr Meyer angrily. "Well," he explained, "we knew that if we told you what she'd said, you would be very angry, so we didn't tell you, but just told the papers anyway." Mr Meyer certainly is a clever man, unlike Mr Hanley who when we returned from South Africa had still only managed to do one clue in his crossword — and even then he had to rub it out because his answer had too many letters. He had written in "Wildebeest" when the right answer was obviously "Gnu".

Thursday

Today I am continuing my week as a world statesman by having a visit from Mr Yeltsin who is the one who is Prime Minister of what used to be called Russia, but is now called something different. Mr Meyer had decided that the highlight of the visit should be a trip to the village pub near Chequers, which used to be called the Buckingham Arms but has now been called the Hedgehog and Bucket. "This is a bit like

Russia," I said to Mr Yeltsin, as I was queuing up to get served, but Mr Yeltsin did not understand. When we had got our drinks and crisps, we went out to have our photograph taken by lots of photographers who were waiting outside, and I gave Mr Yeltsin a cricket bat as a souvenir of England. He made a joke in Russian, which our translator said meant: "I will use it to hit my wife over the head." But he then handed me back the bat, saying something else in Russian. The translator explained that Mr Yeltsin had been hoping for a signed copy of "the famous comedy book by your great English writer Terry Major-Ball". "Mr Yeltsin would not want that," I told him, in my special getting-angry-about-Terry's book voice. "It is full of mistakes." Incidentally, I have found another howler on page 81, when it says that father had bought us two Fair-Isle jumpers for Christmas at Baldwin's in Padmore Road. But as everyone knows Baldwin's had closed down years before that, and our pullovers came from Wallington's opposite the station.

Friday

Today I have decided that it is Mr Mates's turn to go on to the world stage to stick up for Britain. He was the man who had to resign for giving a watch to Mr Nadir, who had given so much money to the Conservative Party. I can't quite remember what was wrong with this, but it was all a long time ago. The point is that he is a respected member of the party and he knows a lot about Ireland, so I thought he was the ideal man to send to America to appear with Mr Adams on all the TV shows and allow the American public to choose between them. In the middle of the night, the telephone rang in our bedroom and an American lady asked whether I would take a "reverse person-to-person call from a Colonel Mates in Wisconsin". Eventually, Mr Mates came on the line saying "Great news, Prime Minister, I'm just about to appear on the Milwaukee Home Shopping Channel's Drive 'n' Weather

Hour." "Oh yes, that's very good," I said. "I hope you're not finding all these programmes too tiring. How many have you been on so far?" At this point Mr Mates had a fit of coughing and the line went dead while a voice said: "That'll be 58 dollars and 37 cents, caller — have a nice day."

Saturday

I have had enough of being successful on the world stage, and have decided it is time to concentrate on home affairs. I am getting not inconsiderably annoyed with Mr Blair, whom I never think about and whom I certainly am not frightened is going to win the next election. Oh no. He is so desperate for votes that he is even promising that he will cut taxes if he wins. How dare he say that, when that is our idea. Everyone knows that we were the first to say that we were going to cut taxes. If Mr Blair won the election, which he won't, he would soon find that he had to put taxes *up* instead, just as we did. He is totally dishonest and certainly does not deserve to win the next election, which he won't. Mr Hanley came in again during the afternoon, to say that he wanted to ask me a very important question. Was there such a word as "Zobic"?

Monday

I am glad to say that the Labour Party conference was a complete flop. Even the *Daily Mail* said so. I was too busy to watch Mr Blair's speech, but when I turned it on he was totally unconvincing. The audience obviously only gave him a standing ovation because they felt sorry for him. He said that he was in favour of lower taxation, private enterprise, law and order and improved standards in education. It is typical of the Labour Party to adopt all these policies just when they have been shown to have hopelessly failed. Our conference will be very different. For a start, Mr Blair smiles all the time. No one will be smiling at our conference. Oh no. And another mistake we will not be making this year. Last year our conference was totally ruined by the woman whom I never mention, who was publicising her book 'The Years of Success Before That Idiot Threw It All Away'. This year I am glad to say we shall have no trouble from her, thank goodness, because she will be in America visiting her son.

Tuesday

I am in no small measure "incandescent with rage", as it said in the *Telegraph*. Mrs Thatcher has done it again. She is on all the front pages looking very depressed because her son has been revealed to have made a lot of money out of arms deals. It is typical of Mrs Thatcher to try and steal the limelight once again just when we're going to have our most successful conference since last year. When my wife Norman and I arrived at Bournemouth, all the reporters asked me what I was going

to do about "sleaze". I said that we were going to privatise it. That soon shut them up!

As I was unpacking my case and putting the trousers of my grey suit in the trouser press, Mr Meyer came in. "That is indeed a coincidence," I said to him. "I was just putting my trousers in the press, when you come in, who are responsible for putting me in the press." "And you both come out equally flat," he said. Obviously he did not understand my joke, but I thought it was good enough to use in my big speech. By the way, I have bought a new book from Ryman's which I have called my "Joke Book", so that I can write down any good jokes I hear to use in my speeches. The joke about Mr Meyer being my "trouser press officer" will be a good start.

In my bath this morning I thought of another joke for the book which was sent to me by my speechwriter Mr Norris Morris. "Q: Why is Mr Blair called Bambi? A: Because when he gets in, he will make everything a little dear."

Anyway Mr Meyer had some good news. "You will not be overshadowed by Lady Thatcher," he said. "Excellent," I said. "No," he said. "You will be overshadowed by Norma Lamont."

Sure enough, when I turned on the hotel television I saw my ex-friend Norma walking along the promenade carrying a clinking plastic bag with the words "Thresher's of Bournemouth" printed on it. Then there was a film of him making a speech at a fringe meeting attended by only a few thousand people. "Now I am no longer in the government," Norma was saying. "I no longer have to tell lies: Europe is a total disaster and we should get out at once." All the people listening to him were so embarrassed by this fearful gaffe, that they clapped and cheered. No one would get away with that sort of rubbish at the main Conference, I told Mr Meyer.

Wednesday

Mr Portaloo today made a speech saying that Europe was a disaster and we should get out at once. There was a deafening roar when he said this, and everyone got up out of their seats ready to leave in protest at him saying anything so stupid. A lot of people were so annoyed that they shouted rude words in Spanish at him, like "Bravo", "Encore" and "The sooner you're in Number 10 the better". Then, I am glad to say, Mr Heseltine made a very sensible and statesmanlike speech, saying that Europe was a jolly good thing and we should stay in it. Everyone was so impressed that they stayed silent at the end for several minutes, thinking about all the wise things he had said.

Thursday

I am getting in no small measure quite irritated by delegates coming up to me at the conference asking me to sign copies of my brother Terry's book, which I haven't read. "I hope you realise," I said to one lady from Haywards Heath, who had bought 16 copies as Christmas presents, "that it is full of mistakes. For example, on page 126, there is a picture of our pet squirrel (Robert, not Cyril, as we all know) which is credited as having been taken by Terry, whereas in fact it was taken by me with the Box Brownie which Auntie Beryl gave me for my eighth birthday. I particularly remember because she got it from Timothy White's the Chemists, in Purley."

Mentioning the squirrel did, however, give me a brilliant idea which I have been telling all the journalists. "I was watching a grey squirrel the other day burying some nuts in the ground," I tell them, "and it reminds me of my government's prudent handling of the economy." My wife Norman said, "You mean, some nondescript little grey creature who's lost his nuts?" "That is not very helpful," I told her, and went up to my room to write my big speech and press my trousers again.

Friday

Today I made my historic speech, which I make every year. This year it was different. "We will tell everyone that you wrote it yourself," said Mr Meyer. "That is a brilliant idea," I said. "Who thought of that?" "Your speechwriter, Mr Norris Morris," he replied.

These were the very important main points of my keynote speech, which I spelt out in no uncertain manner.

● Labour are no good and I am not frightened of Tony Blair.

● We are not divided on Europe so I will not go into it in case I offend anyone.

● We will not abolish the National Health Service because we have already done that.

● Every child over 4 will have a nursery school education, subject to availability.

● I will make everyone rich in the future provided they continue to vote for me.

Also my main slogan, or sound-bite as it is known in this business, was the best I have ever had:

"You don't want someone with a vision. You want an ordinary man in the street wearing a sensible suit and glasses, telling you honestly that he has made a mess of everything but he will try and do better next time."

My wife Norman thought that this was a bit long for a sound-bite and suggested "I resign" as an alternative.

This was again not very helpful as it did not in any measure convey the "feelgood factor" that you need for a successful Conference speech.

It was just as well that I ignored her, as my speech was a huge success.

The clapping went on and on until Mr Hanley told the delegates they could stop. Even Mr Portaloo liked it and he laughed openly all the way through. Even though there were no funny bits in it. In the end I decided not to use my Bambi joke or my trouser-press joke or indeed any others.

"There is one joke too many in this Party already," said Mr Hanley, obviously referring to Mr Heseltine but pointing at me to make sure I knew what he meant.

November

Sunday

At last everything seems to be going my way. Not that it wasn't before. Oh no. But now it most certainly is. I have brought peace to Northern Ireland, which is more than any other prime minister has ever done in the whole of history, including Mr Gladstone, Mr Lloyd George and the woman I never mention, i.e. Mrs Thatcher, with her famous poem by St Francis, "Where there is peace let me sow discord". Anyway, everyone has now agreed to a ceasefire except Mr Paisley, the one who shouts at me and who can therefore be ignored. I have achieved this great triumph without in any way compromising. I told the IRA they had to agree to a permanent ceasefire. And they have now completely agreed, by saying that they will promise to lay down their arms permanently, unless the talks don't go their way. This is good enough for me, so we can now get on with the rest of the Major-Reynolds peace plan, which is to find a way of handing over Northern Ireland to the Irish, but only of course with the full agreement of the people of Northern Ireland.

Monday

Today Parliament resumed, but with a historic difference. Mr Blair and I have agreed that it is time to put an end to the undignified slanging match at Question Time. In the days of some prime ministers, such as Mr Gladstone and my immediate predecessor, the whole thing just became an excuse for the prime minister to shout back at the leader of the opposition, such as Mr Disraeli or Mr Kinnock, and totally humiliate them. But now things are going to be different. Oh yes. Mr Blair has promised not to be nasty to me, and in return I will be nice to him. This is what a mature democracy is all about. For instance, this afternoon Mr Blair said he completely agreed with our policy of implementing the EC's very sensible directive on recycling boxes in supermarkets, 92/342, and I then agreed with him. While we were agreeing, all the MPs were so impressed by this new spirit of harmony that they went off to the bars to celebrate.

Tuesday

Unfortunately, while I was finishing off my Fruit Loops this morning, Mr Meyer rushed in holding a copy of the *Guardian*, which is a newspaper I never read because it is nearly as rude about my government as the *Daily Telegraph*. "Bad news, prime minister," he shouted. "I'm afraid two of your ministers have been caught taking backhanders from the man who runs Harrods." As usual on these occasions, I was of course profoundly shocked. I asked who it was this time. "Smith and Hamilton," said Mr Meyer. I replied that I had never beard of Mr Smith, so he had better resign immediately. But Mr Hamilton was a very important member of my team, and I would therefore give him my full support, as I did previously to Mr Mellor, Mr Lamont, Mr Mates and Mr Yeo. "Hadn't we better find out first whether they are guilty or not?" asked Mr Meyer.

I agreed that we should call in Sir Robin Butler to write a letter saying that all these allegations were totally unfounded, but nevertheless Mr Smith should resign. "That will be the end of the matter," I said. "I have now drawn a line under it."

Wednesday

Once again I am in no small measure furious with the newspapers, who as usual have not realised that I have drawn a line under this matter. All their headlines this morning were the same, "Tide of Sleaze Engulfs Dithering PM". I am not dithering. I am standing firm. I will not change my mind just because of the press.

Thursday

I may have to change my mind. Mr Hamilton has gone too far. This morning I almost choked on my Golden Grahams (which are a not inconsiderably tasty new breakfast cereal) when I heard him on Radio 2 News Roundup comparing himself to *me* at the time when I didn't have an affair with the cook. "This is outrageous," I told my wife Norman. "His situation is entirely different from mine. I was prime minister. But he is just an embarrassment to the government." For some reason, it was then Norman's turn to choke on her Golden Grahams.

At that moment my new friend Sir Robin Butler called up from the mobile phone on his bike as he was cycling in to Whitehall. "Ahem, prime minister," he said. "I think we have a teensy-weensy problem re your friend Mr Hamilton. I respectfully suggest that he may have to become your ex-friend asap." At this point, Sir Robin must have gone under a bridge, as his voice faded away. When I could hear him again, he was saying that the usual solution to this kind of mess was to set up a public enquiry under a judge. "By the time he comes up with his report in two years time," said Sir Robin, "it will all have blown over."

I realised that it was time for me to show people who was running this country, so I did as Sir Robin suggested. I sent a firm fax to Mr Hamilton, telling him that he had decided to resign, and that I, very sadly, had agreed to accept his resignation. Half an hour later he very graciously sent me a reply which read: "You bastard." At last a line has been drawn under the so-called Sleaze Affair.

Friday

Now they are saying that my friend Mr Howard was also approached by Mr Fayed who wanted to become a British citizen. As my wife Norman said: "I can't understand why anyone should want to be a British citizen at a time when the whole country is falling apart." "Obviously," I told her, "you are referring to the Prince of Wales and his articles in the *Sunday Times*. Nevertheless, as I have made clear to the House, Charles will certainly become King." "It is funny," she replied, "how people can make complete fools of themselves these days, and still stay in office."

I rang Mr Howard for a full explanation and he assured me that there wasn't a word of truth in this rumour about him and the man at Harrods. This is good news, as it means I can once again draw a firm line under this sleaze business.

Saturday

The papers are full of some completely unfounded story about one of my new friends Mr Aitken, just because he stayed at the Ritz like Mr Hamilton. I at once rang Mr Aitken to ask him if it was true. "Yes," he said, "but my wife paid the bill."

That really does drawn a line under it this time.

Sunday

I was woken up very early this morning by Mr Aitken.

"Have you read the papers yet?" he asked me. "No," I said. "Good," he continued, "because I've just remembered that my wife only paid half the bill and I paid the rest immediately."

I asked him in my not inconsiderably stern voice if there was anything else he had not told me. Mr Aitken assured me that this was the end of the matter and that line-wise this really was in no small measure drawn now.

Later that morning he rang again. "I've just remembered something else, Prime Minister. I didn't exactly pay the bill immediately. More sort of five months later when Sir Robin asked me about it."

This is why Mr Aitken is such a valuable member of my government. He has a good memory and a fine eye for detail.

Now with his help I can draw a line under all the lines that have already been drawn.

This is the line in question. It is a very thick one and there is no room for anything underneath.

"It is nearly as thick as you lot," said my wife Norman when I showed it to her.

Monday

As I have been trying to make clear to people every day for the past three weeks, the sleaze factor is completely behind me. This was very well shown today when the daily resignation reported in the *Telegraph* was of a Mr Martin (whom I had not heard of) who did not resign because of the sleaze at all. Oh no. He told the reporters: "I am resigning because I want to be free to say that the government is totally incompetent."

This is very good news indeed. It shows that no one is concerned with sleaze any more, and they have now returned to the real issues, i.e. is the government competent or not? Which of course it is. Particularly now the sleaze is over. Oh yes.

Tuesday

We had a very good Cabinet meeting today, when we discussed what the Queen might say in her speech next week. We all agreed that the most important thing we could think of for the future of Britain was to sell off the Post Office. As Mr Clarke explained, this would raise billions of pounds, which would enable him to cut taxes and win us the next election. Mr Heseltine broke off from doing his Canadian Air

Force exercises in the corner to say that this was a very cynical view, and that the real reason for privatising the Post Office was to make it more competitive. "We live in the age of the fax," he said. "No one sends letters any more." To prove it he showed us all hundreds of letters he had received supporting this view. Most of them were from a man called Mr Cockburn who works at the Post Office.

We were just about to vote in favour of this very sensible proposal when Mr Hanley burst into the room. "This is no time to ask us for help with your crossword," I told him in my very stern voice. "This is an important Cabinet meeting, as you can see." But Mr Hanley said nothing, and put six letters on the table in front of me. They were all from Tory MPs saying that they would vote against selling off the Post Office. I was suddenly in no small measure annoyed with Mr Heseltine for trying to win us over to his silly idea. "This is just like your pit closures scheme," I told him. "You will never be prime minister. You make far too many mistakes." "Since when has that stopped someone being prime minister?" he said, doing a Burmese hand-spring, which unfortunately knocked off my glasses.

Wednesday

"Great news, prime minister," said my press man Mr Meyer, "the incompetence factor has been put behind us." He held up the morning's newspapers which showed pictures of my friend Mr Mellor looking very happy because he had been caught out with a blonde lady who was not his wife, but who I still thought looked very nice. "I'm afraid it's back to sleaze," he said. "This is terrible," I replied. "He will have to resign immediately." "But he already has," said Mr Meyer. "So he has," I remembered. What a relief. This means that the government is not affected by this story at all. I explained this to my wife Norman when we were relaxing in front of

her new favourite programme *University Challenge*, with that very rude man from Newsnight.

"Surely if your best friend is caught at it twice in a row, then don't you look a bit silly?" she asked. I could not think of an answer to this, so she said: "I will offer it to the other side for a bonus." This was a very silly remark, as I cannot imagine Mr Blair answering it either.

Thursday

Talking of Mr Blair, which I never do, I cannot help noticing that the only reason why he has a lead of 50 per cent over me in the polls is that he never says or does anything memorable. As I told Mr Meyer: "Perhaps this is the secret of success." For some reason he ran out of the room laughing uncontrollably.

Friday

There is very exciting news from America. The Republicans, who are like the Conservatives, have won their biggest victory for 50 years. "This means that there is a great swing back to the right," I told Norman, as we were eating our microwaved McFayed's Porridge Oats. "It must be a good omen for our party to win the next election." "No," she said, "all it means is that the Americans are fed up with being run by a hopeless idiot, who hasn't got a clue."

Saturday

Mr Meyer came in with some more good news. "It's not the sleaze factor OR the incompetence factor any more," he said. "It's sleaze and incompetence both together this time."

He then showed me two important legal documents with lots of Latin written on them. This is a subject I did not get an 'O' Level in, unlike Mr Hurd and Mr Howard who are actually IN the reports. This just goes to show how much a so-called good education does for you! Oh yes! Anyway, according to the Court of Appeal, Mr Howard has broken the law about compensation to people who have been mugged in order to save money. And Mr Hurd has broken the law by giving money to rich foreign businessmen in Malaysia instead of helping the poor. I do not understand what they have done wrong, but obviously I had no idea what either of them were doing when they were doing whatever it was that was wrong.

Mr Hurd phoned me to say he had been thinking of resigning but that he felt he had a duty to the country to stay on.

"Why?" I said in my new stern anti-sleaze-and-incompetence voice.

"In case I am needed in an emergency when someone else is forced out of Number Ten by a right-wing rebellion over Europe and the party needs a safe pair of hands."

"Thank you," I told him. "I appreciate your loyalty."

Mr Howard did not phone at all, which shows that he is too busy being loyal to me to phone up and tell me he is not going to resign either.

December

Monday

Today we all went to the House of Commons to listen to the Queen's Speech. I'm afraid, in my judgement, it was not quite as good as in previous years. She seems to have no ideas about what the government should do. I put this down to her very understandable worries about her family, and especially Prince Charles who a lot of people are saying is not fit to govern. When I said this to my wife Norman, while we were watching *Cracker*, she said: "Perhaps you should give Charles a few tips then." I said that I was a very busy man, but that I would think about it. One thing I noticed was the Queen left out any mention of selling off the railways, which is Mr Clarke's brilliant way of raising £20 billion, so that we can have some tax cuts in time for the next election. But fortunately when I mentioned this to Mr Clarke he said, "Oh, that's alright, Prime Minister, that's covered by the bit at the end where she said 'My Government will press ahead with its plans to do whatever it likes, whenever it feels like it, without necessarily having to tell the public.' "

Tuesday

At last all our problems are over! Oh, yes. We have discovered who has been responsible for everything that has gone wrong for my government in the past four years. It is all the fault of my now ex-friend Miss Hogg, who thought up every single one of my worst ideas, including:

● The Cones Hotline.
● Back to Basics.
● Joining the ERM.
● Not leaving the ERM when we should have.
● Trying to rejoin the ERM.
● Privatising the Post Office.
● Not privatising the Post Office.
● Telling me to appoint Mr Hanley as Chairman after I met him in the tea room and he gave me a signed photo of his mother in *Genevieve*.

Wednesday

All the papers are agreed that I was quite right to sack Miss Hogg. "Major Looks For Scapegoat" said the *Daily Mail*.

The Times was equally supportive with its headline: "Too Little Too Late As Timid Major Fires Top Aide". The *Sun* put it with its usual jokiness: "Dopey John Dumps Cone Woman As Tories Go Down Toilet".

Thursday

I have had a very odd letter from a Mr Maples, who works for Mr Hanley, helping him with the crossword. It was marked "For PM Only — How To Win The Next Election". In it Mr Maples said that he had done a survey of all our supporters in the country — well over 1,000 people — and they had said the following things:

● John Major is useless.
● So are the rest of the Cabinet.
● We don't believe in the recovery.
● We are fed up with sleaze, corruption, lies,

BUY NOW
WHILE
ROLLING
STOCK
LASTS

Europe, privatisation and everything else the government stands for.

● We are particularly angry that the government never listens to anything we say.

I have decided to ignore all this, as it is obviously rubbish.

Unfortunately, when I gave the letter back to Mr Hanley and told him to "chuck it out", he thought I meant send it to all the newspapers. When I read it in the *Daily Telegraph* I noticed that there was even a PS. which I had not bothered to read. This said, "PS. I think our only hope of winning the next election is to get some Tory yobboes to beat up Mr Blair." It is very annoying of Mr Maples to say this. It implies that I am not perfectly well able to beat up Mr Blair myself, as I do twice every week at Question Time. I have only to open my ring-binder for Mr Blair to put on that silly smile and look terrified. For example, only yesterday Mr Blair asked me why I did not resign. I immediately fired back "Because I am the Prime Minister." That shut him up. All he was able to reply was "Not for long, you're not" and all the House laughed at his discomfiture.

Friday

Although I have got rid of Miss Hogg, my problems are not completely over. Apparently, my government is going to be defeated by some Conservative MPs over the European budget. But I have a not inconsiderably clever plan which will totally outwit them. I have told all our MPs that if they don't back me, I shall order the Queen to call an election. And then they will all lose their seats except me, because I have the biggest majority in the country. So I will be the only Conservative MP in Parliament and therefore Leader of the Opposition like Mr Blair. And then I will be popular again. Oh yes. Mr Clarke has brought in his budget, which is almost as clever as my Budgets used to be when I was Chancellor.

Mr Clarke is going to raise taxes so that he can lower them again before the next election. "The more I put them up, the more I can bring them down," he explained.

"It may make you unpopular in the short term, but it will make whoever is Prime Minister next year very popular indeed," he said cheerfully. "Particularly if he is a former Chancellor."

This I took as a not inconsiderable compliment to myself.

Unfortunately, he left his red box behind and also a number of suitcases and trunks labelled "K. Clarke, No. 10 Downing Street. To await arrival."

Saturday

My very ex-friend Norma Lamont wants to be Prime Minister, I read in the *Daily Telegraph*.

How ungrateful can you get?

Anyway, Norma does not seem to have noticed that there is already a Prime Minister in office, ie me. "Don't worry. No one will vote for him," my wife Norman assured me. "He was the one that ran *your* leadership campaign."

Women are never very logical in their attitude to politics (see Mrs Thatcher), but I think she may have a point this time.

Sunday

Good news at last! Though not very good news for my in-no-small-measure ex-friend Norma Lamont. The newspapers now agree that he has no chance of being Prime Minister! No indeed! It is going to be Mr Heseltine, or Mr Portillo, or Mr Clarke or Mr Howard or, as they put it, "*any* member of the current cabinet except one". (Probably Mr Waldegrave.)

That certainly will take the fizz out of Mr Lamont's cheap champagne from Threshers*. Oh yes.

The Proprietor's name at Threshers is a Mr Onanoogoo, and not, as my brother Terry keeps telling reporters at first nights and film premieres, Mr Hargreaves. Terry has mixed him up with the man who used to own the chemist's on the corner of Parkdown Road all those years ago.

Monday

Today is the historic debate on the European budget. It will be a very important vote, unless of course we lose, in which case it will only be a technical hiccup. My friend Mr Clarke has explained that the money we are giving to Brussels is only a very small amount, although he could not remember the exact figure. And anyway I gave my solemn word to Mr Herr Kohl and Mr Monsieur Mitterrand in 1992 that they could have whatever they liked, to prove that we are at the heart of Europe and in the fast lane, although of course we are going slowly. As I explained to my wife Norman: "I can hardly reverse backwards down the fast lane when everyone behind me is hooting and flashing their lights, can I?" "Why don't you just do a U-turn?" she said. "That's what you normally do." I carried on eating my Kellogg's Honey Frostrups in silence, although I did say that I was treating the vote as a matter of confidence in my government. "I have every confidence that you will lose," she said jokingly.

Tuesday

Norman was right about that silly and totally unimportant vote, which will not bring down my government. Oh no. Just because I lost the vote does not mean that people do not want to vote for me. Oh no! I still have the confidence of almost everyone, except eight so-called conservatives who are in no small measure Loonies, Bastards, Barmies, Traitors and SEVERAL DOZEN APPLES, PEARS AND BANANAS SHORT OF A PICNIC — which no one would invite them to anyway because they are all BASTARDS. I immediately called in my friend Mr Ryder, who is the Chief Whip, and told him that they could no longer be my friends and that he must take away their party whip. "But prime minister," he said, "that means that they will no longer have to vote for the government." "They don't anyway," I said, "because they are Bastards. But now we have punished them, they will soon fall into line. You just wait." Mr Ryder opened the window and jumped out, just like Mr Lamont used to do before he became my ex-friend and the biggest BASTARD AND LOONY OF THEM ALL!

Wednesday

Everything is completely back to normal, I am glad to say. For instance, the Tory newspapers have gone back to their proper job of attacking the Labour Party and Mr Blair. This is because he wants to send his son to a private school so that

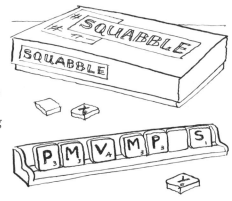

he can get lots of 'O' Levels. Personally, I cannot see why he is going to all this trouble when you don't need any 'O' Levels to get to the top in my new Classless Britain! And the Labour Party have made another terrible blunder by calling for a "slimmed-down" Royal Family like they have in Denmark where the Queen rides round on a bicycle and stays married to her husband. This will make Mr Blair's party even more unpopular, as is shown by the *Daily Mail's* poll, which says that only 78 per cent are in favour of the kind of monarchy Labour are suggesting.

Thursday

I am not inconsiderably worried about the very worrying situation in the Republic of Ireland. It seems that there is no clear leadership, the government no longer has a majority and there is not even a proper prime minister. We are very lucky in Britain that we do not live in Ireland, oh yes.

Friday

Today is another historic day, when we shall show who is in charge in this country by our vote to put VAT on domestic fuel, as we were told to by Brussels. Not that I can reveal this because it is a secret. In public I tell everyone that this brilliant idea is completely my own. I am confident that we will have a very good majority on this one. The so-called rebels will support us because they are so keen to get back into my good books, and out of those other books, e.g. the ones from Ryman's with "Loonies" and "Bastards" written on them. Also, the Ulster Unionists will definitely vote for me, after all I have done to bring peace to Northern Ireland.

Saturday

Unfortunately, we didn't quite get enough votes last night, but considering that we are now a minority party we did exceedingly well. Mr Lamont's ridiculous idea of putting VAT on fuel was never a very good one in the first place, and this vote is really a victory for common sense and shows how right I was to sack him.

Fortunately, I was able to forget about such trivial matters, as I had to play my part on the world stage by flying off to a place called Budapest, which is in Hungary, for a conference to bring peace to Bosnia, which I don't think is in Hungary. Mr Hurd told me on the plane that the conference was called OSCEOD, or possibly it was CODSECO. Anyway, it was a very important meeting and we all reached full agreement on the fact that we could not agree on anything. This was because there were too many countries and there was not enough time. As Mr Hurd said, the conference had been "very helpful" and was "a very significant step forward". Mr Yeltsin shouted something in Russian and fell over, which is obviously the Russian way of saying "we agree".

Monday

My friend Mr Clarke has come up with another brilliant Budget. That is two in one week, which is not inconsiderably impressive. To make up for the money we will not get from VAT on fuel he has decided to put up the prices of cigarettes, petrol and drink. It is a very clever idea. My only question was: "Why did you not do that before?" He replied, quick as a flash: "Because it would have made the Government unpopular." I had not thought of this, but Mr Clarke, as ever, had his finger on the pulse. "Everyone will now blame the rebels for making all their luxuries more expensive," he told me. "*They* will be the unpopular ones now." "Oh yes," I said. "We can blame them if we lose the by-election this week too." "Brilliant!" said Mr Clarke. "Have you ever thought of being Prime Minister?" Then he added, with a laugh: "I have."

Tuesday

Today I am sending out Christmas cards to all my friends. My list is rather shorter than last year because I do not send cards to BASTARDS, LOONIES or BARMIES!! Oh no! I am also seriously considering crossing off my brother Terry. He has sent me a Christmas card with a picture of himself and someone called Mariella Frostrup, who is a film star I think. Underneath the picture it reads: "Look what a cracker I've pulled!" Celebrity has clearly gone to his head and I refuse to put this silly card on the mantelpiece next to my other card (from Jeffrey Archer).

Wednesday

I see that I am coming to the end of another diary and I am still prime minister. Oh yes! Whatever anyone else says, I am still here. I did get rather a shock when Mr Hanley rushed into my office shouting "Terrible news, prime minister! We've lost Dudley West," "Oh no," I said. "What's happened to him? How did he die? I hope this isn't going to mean another by-election."

Fortunately Mr Hanley explained that Dudley West was a constituency where Labour had just won the seat by a huge landslide. "That will teach the Euro-rebels," I said at once. "It shows they have no support in the country at all." Mr Hanley at once agreed with my analysis. "Quite right, prime minister. That is just what I told Sue and John this morning, not to mention Anne and Nick and Richard and Judy. Oh, and Kilroy." 'I am not interested in what you told your friends," I said in my stern 'I'm-in-charge' voice. "Your job is to go on radio and TV and tell the nation that the Euro-rebels are bastards."

Thursday

Let one thing be clear. I have had enough of these Euro-rebels. Now they are calling for a referendum. How absurd. That is not our way. However, that is not to say that I would rule it out. Nor that I would rule it in. It is possible that I might even decide to allow a referendum on whether we should have a referendum. This should shut the rebels up. On the other hand, I might just decide not to have a referendum on a referendum. That is not necessarily our way. After all, I have been elected to give this country a lead and to act decisively. Oh yes. Or oh no, as the case may be.

Friday

I have been thinking a lot recently about whether we should have a referendum or not. There is a lot to be said for it, whatever the Euro-rebels may say. But the problem is to decide what the question should be. I have drafted a possible wording with the help of my adviser Morris Norris.

Q.Do you really want the total disorder of a Labour government which would put up taxes, abolish the monarchy, allow the trade unions to run riot and leave millions of bodies unburied in the street?

A. Yes/No.

This should do the trick. It will certainly annoy Mrs Thatcher who has called me a 'wimp' today in the *Daily Telegraph*. I only know this because my wife Norman cut it out and stuck it to the fridge door with one of those little magnets with a tiger on them that you get with Kellogg's new Sugar-Coated Frostrups. When you collect six of them, you can send off for a large furry tiger. We have now collected five, so there is only one to go. Anyway, Mrs Thatcher is completely wrong, as usual. A wimp would not have had the courage to kick out eight MPs from his own party, like I did. I told Norman that Mrs Thatcher would never have done that. "No," she said, "because they would have been too scared to rebel against her."

Thinking about it, a big tiger would be a bit frightening to have sitting on the kitchen table if you came down in the middle of the night to fetch a glass of water.

Saturday

Very soon now it will be time for our three-week Christmas recess. But before we have our holiday, we have managed to put through a very important and historic piece of legislation, the MPs (To Work Fewer Hours) Bill 1994. As I explained to Norman, "I will be spending much more time at home next year." "All day and every day, I imagine," she replied, obviously not having bothered to read the details of the bill at any considerable length.

Christmas Eve

It is Christmas Eve. This morning my brother Terry brought round my present, which looks suspiciously like a book. If it is the one I think it is, it would be very considerably in no small measure annoying since he knows quite well that I have told him that I am much too busy to read it.

"You cannot take it

back," he joked, "as it has been signed by the author." Then he had to leave, to appear on the Xmas With Sky Star Special. "I am going to be on with Chris Eubank and Julie Goodyear who is Bet in *Coronation Street*," he said. "I am too busy to know about these things," I replied, but he had already gone.

Christmas Day

We had a quiet Christmas with all our friends, i.e. Jeffrey Archer. After tea we played Scrabble and Jeffrey won, although I couldn't help noticing that Norman wrote all his words for him. I thought this was strange, since he is such a world-famous author. This was the final score: Major, J. 3 points. Major, N. (my wife) 164. Archer, J. (Lord) 3,612. Scorer: J.A.

New Year's Eve

Tonight Norman and I joined hands and sang a song to see in the New Year (at 9.30 p.m. no less!). The words are very silly as I am unlikely to forget any of my "auld acquaintances". Oh no. They are all written down in a new book called "Auld Bastards".

January 1995

New Year's Day

It says in the paper that I am going to retire and become a banker like Mr Lamont. Not many people know that before I became Prime Minister I was actually a Senior Bank Officer with very serious responsibilities indeed, e.g. making sure the biros still had chains on and sticking the little numbers on the Foreign Exchange window. I can honestly say that I never lost a single plastic number, unlike Mr Jarvis who replaced me who once listed the US dollar as being worth 5p!!!

Needless to say there is not a single mention of this in a certain book I got for Christmas but which I am never going to mention again, i.e. Terry's.

Sunday

I was very sad to see that the great cricketer P.B.H. May has passed away (I have his autograph on my school bat next to that of C.P. Snedding who was the Games Master). Peter May was an amateur. "There are not enough amateurs in charge," I said to Norman over our Cocoa-Pops. "Oh, I don't know," she replied, smiling in her funny way.

Monday

Another very successful year is just beginning. I am now the 25th longest serving prime minister of all time. I have already passed Mr Callaghan, Mr Heath and the Marquess of Aberdeen. At least, this is what I have been told by my speech writer Mr Norris. Soon I will have been here longer than Mr Gladstone, Mr Pitt the Younger and even, dare I say it, the woman whose name I never mention — all I have to do is win the next two elections, as I will. Oh yes. I gave a special New Year message to the Party to cheer them up. Not that they need cheering up. Oh no. I told them, in the words of Mr Norris, that the "feelgood factor" is just round the corner, at the end of the tunnel, and that the Government is actually nowhere near as unpopular as everyone says.

I was in no small measure pleased to see that my ex-friend Miss Hogg has become Lady Hogg in the new classless Honours List. It is quite wrong for people to say that she was only made a Lady as consolation for me sacking her. We do not do things like that. It is not our way. Otherwise Mr Lamont would now be Lady Lamont, which would be ridiculous!

Tuesday

The so-called "New" Labour Party are pathetic, and are showing that they completely have feet of straw, in my judgement. Within hours of announcing that they would put VAT on school fees, Mr Blair announced that they would not, after all. "They are behaving just like you," said my wife Norman, as we were eating our new M & S Euro-croissants with almond and date filling. "No," I told her, "we have never said that we would put VAT on school fees,"

although it is quite a good idea when you think about it. It would annoy Mr Hurd, Mr Waldegrave and Mr Blair, who all went to public schools!

Wednesday

Mr Howard has come in yet again to not offer me his resignation. This time he has let lots more prisoners escape, just like Sir Norman Fowler used to do from his Group 4 vans. But Mr Howard had a very good explanation. "It is not my fault," he said. "The Prison Service has now become a Next Steps Agency, i.e. a semi-autonomous, non-accountable body." "What does that mean?" I asked him. "It means that it is not my fault," he said. After he left I wondered whether we could have one of these agencies to take over the government. Then I wouldn't have to resign if things went wrong, which they haven't. Oh no.

Thursday

There is a silly story in the newspapers saying that a top-secret new committee has been set up of 12 "wise men (and women)" to stop me making mistakes. This cannot be true, since I do not make any mistakes. To confirm this I asked all the twelve members of my new advisory committee whether they could think of any mistakes I had made. They were all silent for quite a long time, which proves they could not think of any.

After the meeting Mr Hanley came in shouting: "A great new plan to win us the election." "How many letters?" I asked him. "No, prime minister," he said. "It's not the crossword. It is a list of all the terrible things that happened when we last had a Labour government. All we have to do is read out my list on television and no one will ever want to vote for Mr Blair again." "Alright," I said, "let us pretend that *I* am the electorate, and *you* are me reading it out on a party political broadcast." He began to read. "First, the three-day week. Oh no, sorry, forget that one. Secondly, the huge killer rats roaming the streets while millions of dead bodies lay unburied because the dustmen were on strike?"

"Brilliant," I said. "I will never vote Labour again."

Friday

As usual I stayed up all night listening to the very exciting news of the Test Match. I must say, the press look very silly, having said that we were a hopeless team of no-good incompetents, led by a complete wimp. In fact, Mr Atherton and his team have pulled off a historic draw, which shows that you should not write people off just because they are no good.

Saturday

Mr Poraloo has made another of his speeches in which he tries to become Leader of the Party. This time he pretended his speech was about Ethics — not the county where I am very popular!! — but the fact that people cannot tell the difference between right and wrong.

"Or extreme right and wrong," said my friend Mr Clarke at our routine weekend Cabinet meeting. This made everybody laugh except Mr Portaloo. And me, because I did not understand what he meant.

"The difference is that I am right and Mr Portaloo is wrong," I explained in my new stern putting-our-house-in-order voice. This time Mr Portaloo laughed very loudly.

Sunday

Today I was on Sir David Frost's television programme and I was the main guest — not just reviewing the newspapers, oh no! Sir David wanted to ask me my opinion about all kinds of important issues of the day. Luckily I knew the answers to every one because Mr Meyer, my press officer, had written them down for me beforehand.

"I am ruling out a referendum until I have to have one," I told him in my ruling-things-out voice.

Sir David was speechless, but my next answer made him even more speechless.

"And if the rebels keep voting against me I'm going to give them the Whip back."

After the show Sir David congratulated me on my "super, wonderful" performance. "You really showed everyone that you are a man who knows his own mind," he said. "Do you think so?" I replied. "I'm not sure."

Monday

Today I decided to have a historic press conference to unveil my plans for winning the next election. "What are they?" asked my press adviser Mr Meyer. "That is your job," I told him. "I cannot be expected to do everything". A few hours later he came in with a piece of paper on which he had written the following ideas:

1. Labour is hopelessly divided over Europe.
2. Their policy on rail privatisation is embarrassing.
3. Er...
4. Vote Conservative.

The press conference was a great success. Lots of famous journalists were there and after I had explained how well the government was doing, some of them even asked questions. One asked: "If the government is doing so well, why has your poll rating fallen to 2 per cent?" I immediately replied, quick as a flash: "The Royal Family are the glue that holds the nation together." I could see they were very surprised by this brilliant answer, which I had thought up earlier when I was in Ryman's purchasing some new notebooks. I had noticed how many different types of glue there were, i.e. UHU, Pritstik, Loctite, Bostik and many others. I thought how important glue was, and I remember how in the old days we used Gripfix to mend the gnomes when their heads fell off. For some reason Terry does not mention this in his famous book, probably because many of the ones which broke were made by him, i.e. not very well. Anyway, it was very clever of me to mention the Queen, as it made the journalists forget

about "rebels" like Mrs Gorman, who has now got a notebook all of her own called "Bastards (Female)". She is the only entry in the book apart from the woman I never mention who is mentioned under "T".

Tuesday

Today is another historic day, as my enemy Mr Monsieur Delors has finally resigned from running Europe. I have been working towards this for five years, and now a very different man has replaced him, i.e. my new friend Mr Monsieur Santer. He supports all my policies, as he made clear in his opening speech. "Mesdames and messieurs," he said. "Vive la nouvelle Europe. Vive le federalisme. Vive l'ecu. À bas cette prat gris Anglais, avec ses idées stupide de subsidiarité. Pah! Merde. Vive la France. Deutschland über alles." I admit that I did not understand every word of this, as I do not have 'O' Level French like Mr Hurd, who I asked to translate the bits I didn't understand, i.e. all of it. Mr Hurd told me that the speech "lost a lot in translation", but that there was nothing very new in it and it marked no shift in our policy.

Wednesday

The papers have got it wrong as usual. They are all trying to make out that Mr Santer was somehow being rude about me in his speech. This just goes to show that they do not speak French as well as Mr Hurd! The Labour people pathetically tried to use this in the House of Commons, asking me whether I still "believed in Santer". "Of course I do," I said. "He is the glue that binds Europe together, just like the Queen." That stopped Labour laughing, until they started again. But I wasn't finished yet. When I turned over the next page of my ringbinder, there was another of my brilliant jokes written by my special new jokewriter, Mr James. "If they mention Santer," he told me, "try this one." So I did. "Perhaps the Right Honourable Leader of the Opposition could tell us at this point whether he still believes in Santer Clause 4?" All our side thought this was the most brilliant joke they had ever heard, and Mr Ryder stood up holding a card which said: "Laugh loudly or I shall withdraw the whip." The cheering and clapping went on for a not inconsiderable number of minutes, and in my judgement it was my greatest triumph ever in the House of Commons.

Thursday

Today I had another amazing triumph when I won the

great fish debate by a huge majority, i.e. 3. All the papers had been predicting that I would lose, thanks to the Bastards and Loonies, i.e. Mrs Gorman and Sir Richard Body who is the one who has been let out of a mental hospital under my Community Care policy. I told Mr Waldegrave to say that the government would now pay millions of pounds to our

fishermen to stay at home watching TV, so that the Spanish could catch all the fish around the shores of Britain. That kept most of our people happy, and then to make sure of winning the vote I sent a message to my friends the Ulster Unionists. "If you keep my government in power," I said, "I'll see you right, and furthermore I give you my solemn assurance that any Catholic fish caught crossing the border into Ulster will be immediately extradited." No wonder we won. The Bastards and Loonies are no match for me. If I want to surrender to Europe I will not be defeated by my own side. Oh no.

Friday

My new National Lottery is going extremely well and we now have a very considerable amount of money to give to worthy causes. Mr Clarke asked if the Conservative Party could have some of it but I had to say no. "My own top priority is to encourage young people to be more competitive at games," I said. "That's a good idea," said Mr Portaloo as he and Mr Heseltine raced the length of the Cabinet Room to see who could get to my chair first.

Sunday

My idea of competition seems to be catching on. Mr Blair went on television trying to imitate me by giving an interview to my friend Sir David Frost (who I gave a knighthood because he is my friend).

My wife Norman and I watched Mr Blair at home and
Norman said: 'He is nearly as boring as you" — i.e. I was the
best. To celebrate this new competitive victory I had another
bowl of Banana Bubbles, which are now my favourite cereal.
Oh yes.

Mr Blair was particularly unimpressive on the subject of
Clause Four. He got really flustered as Mr Frost kept asking
him more and more questions which he could not answer.

"No one that stupid could ever win an election," I said after
drinking the banana-flavoured milk left after you have eaten
the cereal (which is in my judgement why this cereal is in no
small measure superior to other cereals).

Norman gave me one of her funny looks.

February

Monday

Today was a very unhistoric day when we had a routine
emergency Cabinet meeting about Europe. Not that there
was an emergency, oh no. Nor that we have changed our
policy. The policy is what it is always been, e.g. that we
should be at the heart of Europe driving in the fast lane. Only
this time we have made it very clear that we will be driving
in the opposite direction to everyone else. This is because Mr
Hanley had read a poll in the *Daily Telegraph* which was on
the same page as his crossword, saying that 92 per cent of the
country was now worried by Europe and thought that the
Euro-sceptics might have a point. Well, we can be Euro-
sceptics too, I said, quick as a flash, only Euro-sceptics at the
heart of Europe, being sceptical in the fast lane. For a minute
or two the Cabinet was silent, as they thought about my
brilliant new policy, which is not new but the same one we
have always had. Oh yes. Then Mr Portaloo burst out
laughing and said: "Glad you have decided to join us, John.
Does that mean we are all what you call Bastards now?"
Everyone joined in the good-natured spirit of this joke, and
shouted "You bastard," pointing at me.

Tuesday

I was not inconsiderably annoyed this morning to hear
both Mr Heath and Mr Lord Howe on the radio saying that I
was a traitor. How dare they? I have been prime minister for

much longer than Mr Heath, and Mr Lord Howe was never even prime minister at all. It takes real leadership to stand up and drive the wrong way in the fast lane, with all your lights flashing. Mr Hurd also was not pleased when one of the rebels said that, now that we're all Euro-sceptics, he was "yesterday's man". He immediately went on

the television to say that this was quite untrue. He was today's man, and tomorrow's man, and even the day after tomorrow's man. And that he was also a passionate European, whether for or against.

Wednesday a.m.

I was very pleased this morning when the *Times* printed as its main news item my historic peace plan for Ireland, even though we haven't finished it yet. The article said that I was planning the following initiatives:

1. A joint all-Ireland tourist board, split into two sections, one for the North and the other for the South.

2. A joint all-Ireland Cheese Board, to promote cheeses from both sides of the cheese border in the new European Single-Market.

3. Northern and Southern Ireland to be joined by road and rail links.

4. Members of North and South to speak a common language.

5. Eire...

6. That's it.

Just as I was coming to the end of the article, a small man came bursting through my door and started to scream at me, saying: "It's all up, Major, you're finished." He turned out to be someone called Mr Molyneaux from Northern Ireland. "Ah," I said, remembering who he was. "You are one of the nice MPs who always vote to keep me in office, even though you are not Conservatives." "Not any more, Judas," he said, getting my name wrong rather rudely, "you're on your own now." "What do you mean?" I said. "The deal was," he explained, "that we would only keep you in power so long as you preserve the Union. I tell you, Major, you've got just 24 hours to sort this one out." He stormed out.

Wednesday p.m.

After lunch I rang Mr Hurd to tell him what I was going to do. "What shall I do?" I said. "You've got to go on television and tell everyone to keep calm. I'll get one of our people to send over something for you to read out. The main thing is not to panic." "But surely," I said, "if I go on and say 'Don't panic' everyone will think I am panicking, just like Corporal Jones in *Dad's Army*." "*Dad's Army*?" said Mr Hurd, in his typical toffee-nosed way. "What is that?" I had to explain that it was a very popular programme about a hopeless bunch of incompetents who are trying to stop England being taken over by foreigners. They are led by a pompous twit in spectacles who used to work in a bank, who is always having to be told what to do by his upper-class Number Two. "Sounds familiar," said Mr Hurd and rang off.

Thursday,

My historic broadcast on Ireland went down very well. For the record, this is what I told the nation:

"Do not panic. This is not an emergency, which is why I am making this emergency broadcast. I appeal to you all to stay calm, as I am doing. Oh yes. There is absolutely nothing to worry about. Try to look calm and reassuring, John, but don't read this bit out".

Obviously my speech was, in my judgement, a great success. When I came out afterwards everyone in the streets was completely calm, and carrying on just as if nothing had happened.

ANGLO – IRISH PRODUCTION

MUCH ADO ABOUT ALL OR NOTHING

Friday

Mr Molyneaux says that he is no longer my friend and will support Mr Blair instead. This is very silly because Mr Blair agrees with *me* about Northern Ireland. So this will change nothing — except there will be a General Election. Mr Hanley pointed out in the Cabinet meeting that the Conservative Party has got no money and cannot afford to fight an election anyway.

"Why don't we just concede it?" said Mr Portaloo. "And save the money for the next one, when we will have a leader that people might vote for."

Saturday

The newspapers are trying to make out that the Cabinet are divided over a common European currency. Mr Aitken said: "The Ecu will happen over my dead body." Mr Heseltine said: "We should go full steam ahead with the Ecu."

My own position, however, is clear. I agree with both of them. So what is all this talk about a divided Cabinet?

Sunday

It seems I had an affair with an older woman when I was young. My brother Terry did not mention this in his book, which just shows how hopeless Terry is at writing books about me. Oh yes.

As another example Terry claims that I kept breaking gnomes in the workshop and he had to mend them! I did not have time to break gnomes as I was round at No. 27 Burton Road, having tea with my friend Mrs Kierans and showing her my cigarette cards of famous cricketers.

She was very nice and told me that one day I could get to the very top and could even become Branch Manager of a local bank like Mr Mainwaring in the TV series.

Monday

I was not inconsiderably sorry to see all the news placards this morning. They all had in very big letters "NEW TORY SEX SCANDAL". "Oh dear," I said to Mr Hanley. "Who is it this time?" "I am afraid it is you, prime minister," he replied, with a smile. He then read out an article in the *Daily Mail* which had the headline "It was Ovaltine and Love Romps At Number 21". Apparently a long time ago I had a girl friend who has now told all the newspapers about me. However, I do not have to resign because I was not married at the time, unlike Mr Mellor, Mr Yeo and all the others.

Tuesday

My wife Norman is not talking to me. She has been

reading the *Daily Mail*. "I am not talking to you," she said.
"You only married me apparently because you wanted to be
prime minister." "Aha!" I said, in the voice I use when I am
catching out Mr Blair at Question Time. "So you *are* talking
to me." At this she went off in a huff. No wonder I became
prime minister! Then the telephone rang. It was my brother
Terry. "If it is about your appearance at the *Oldie* lunch with
Mr Wogan and Mr Milligan, I am not at all interested," I said.
"I have not even read about it in all the newspapers." "No,"
said Terry. "it's about your affair with that lady from across
the road who Mum didn't like. The papers have been ringing
me up, but I have told them there was not a word of truth in
it. You only played Scrabble together and listened to *Round
the Horne*." "You have got it wrong again, Terry," I said. "Just
like you did in your book when you said on page 124 that I
painted all the gnomes with red hats when father had asked
for blue ones. You know perfectly well that Mr Webster
ordered the red ones and then changed his mind." "There is
no need to take that tone with me," said Terry, "just because
you think that you're important. If you want to be personal,
let me tell you that I have been on television more times than
you this week. And, what is more, I could easily have put in
my book about the time you came back home late from Mrs
Kierans' once, with your pullover on back to front and your
hair all messy." "I did not do anything that night," I told him
very angrily. "I had only taken my jersey off because Mrs
Keirans had put both bars of her fire on and it was very hot."
"Alright then," said Terry, "explain the time when you told
Mum you were going off to play cricket and never came home.
She had to go out looking for you in the street, shouting
'John, John, your tea's getting cold.' " In my judgement, I had
had enough of this silly conversation and I slammed down the
phone just like Mr Paisley does to me.

Wednesday

Today Mr Hanley came in looking very glum. "Another one
down," he said. "I have not got time to help you with your
crossword," I told him. "I have got a not inconsiderable crisis
over Europe to sort out." "No, prime minister," said Mr
Hanley. "I meant another one of your ministers has resigned."
"Oh dear," I said. "Not more sex scandals? This is the last
thing we want." "No," said Mr Hanley, "nothing like that this
time. Mr Wardle has resigned on a matter of principle."
"Phew!" I said. "That's all right then."

The *Daily Mail* is still going on about Mrs Kierans' and me eating chips together. You would think they had something better to write about, like say a split in the Cabinet — not that there is one. Oh no.

Thursday

I am in no small measure fed up with my Cabinet, who are still giving interviews about the Common European Currency. Every time you turn on the television, there are

Mr Hurd, Mr Redwood or Mr Clarke giving completely different views. I will not stand for this, as I told the Cabinet at a special emergency meeting I called to tell them I would not stand for it. "You must stick to the Cabinet line." I told them. "Well, what is our line, Prime Minister?" asked Mr Portalooo, with a clever dick little grin on his face. "I have made our line crystal clear," I told him. "Our line is that we do not have a line at the moment, because it would be quite wrong. But I cannot rule out the possibility of having one sometime in the future, when the time is right." At this there was a long silence, while they all thought how cleverly I had evaded the Euro-crisis. Then Mr Portaloo asked: "Should we send Waldegrave out for some chips — and you could show us all what your policy is with regard to putting vinegar on them?" I had no idea what this was about, but Mr Gummer giggled and said he was "a salt-first man".

Friday

This is the third day Norman has not spoken to me, although when it was time for our tea in front of *The Private Life of Plants*, which is her favourite programme after *Casualty*, she broke her silence. "At least the plants keep their lives private," she said, throwing a bag of chips at me. "There's your chips, just like you and your old flame used to like them!" she spat. I had just finished picking up the chips when the phone rang. It was my brother Terry. "I'm in the radio car, John," he said, "at Radio Talk Chigwell, doing a phone-in on the great Chips Issue, but I can't remember how you did it? Was it salt first and then vinegar, or the other way?" "I am very busy," I told him. "I have not got time to discuss chips with you". "That's OK, John," he said, "I've just given all the listeners your private number, so you can tell them yourself."

Saturday

The Cabinet have taken my instructions to heart. Today there have been no speeches on Europe by Ministers. There have only been speeches by my ex-friend Norma Lamont, my ex-friend Mr Baker and my very-ex-friend Lord Howe. They are however of no importance and no one except the newspapers and television took any notice of them.

Sunday

It is in no small measure annoying the way the media continue to pretend that the Cabinet is split over Europe. I told a reporter today that he should in my judgement ask me questions about important subjects — like the common currency.

Mr Clarke is beginning to not be my friend anymore. He keeps saying that as Chancellor he is "his own man". This is clearly untrue as I am the one who is his own man — i.e. mine, not his.

I told Norman not to invite him round for drinks and furthermore to ring him up and tell him that he was not invited. Mr Clarke said he could not come anyway because he was preparing a big speech on how good it would be to have the ecu.

"If this carries on," I said to Norman, "one of us will have to go."

"Shall I start packing, dear?" she asked, which was rather odd since we have no plans to go on holiday.

March

Monday

Oh dear. This morning we heard the terrible news that one of this country's finest and most respected institutions has collapsed overnight. It is Ryman's the stationers, renowned throughout the world for its high-quality stationery, rubber bands, staplers and ring-binders. Not to mention, of course, little books which are very useful for writing in the names of certain persons, e.g. Bastards, Barmies and the new woman whose name I never mention, i.e. Mrs Gorman. I hear that even her Majesty buys her stationery at Ryman's. When I heard the news I thought it was inconceivable that we should let such a not inconsiderable part of our heritage go bankrupt. So I immediately looked up the number of the Bank of England in the phone book. Having been in banking myself, I knew the ropes and I asked to speak to the manager. "I'm sorry," said a rather rude young woman, "he's in a very important meeting with the Chancellor of the Exchequer discussing the crisis." "Oh good," I said. "That means they are already at work on this terrible news about Ryman's. Don't interrupt them. Just say that John Major called." "And where shall I say you're from?" she asked. "Brixton," I replied. "Not that it's anything to do with you." But for once I put the phone down feeling that the country was in good hands.

Tuesday

Today I was in my very top form at Question Time. For weeks Mr Blair has been asking me the same question. "Does the Prime Minister not deplore the obscene pay rises which are given to bosses of recently nationalised public utilities?" Usually I say, "Oh no, it is entirely a matter for them how much they pay themselves." But today I really made him look a complete dimwit, which is what he is, i.e. a dimwit. He

jumped up with his silly smile and asked his question. Imagine his surprise when I said, "Oh yes. I do deplore the rises. In my judgement they are most distasteful." He was so amazed by my new get-tough policy on pay rises, that all he could do was stand there and ask me what I was going to do about it. Unfortunately I had not thought of that bit, but Mr Hunt passed me a piece of paper with a brilliant reply. "Tell him there's a committee looking into it, and it would be quite improper to pre-empt its findings." There were huge cheers from our side when I read this out, and shouts of "dimwit, dimwit!" even from the Labour side, which shows what a great triumph I had won.

Wednesday

Today is another ordinary historic day when I have to unite the party on Europe with one of my inspiring, agenda-setting speeches. Mr Hurd tells me that what everyone is waiting for is a firm line on (a) the Referendum and (b) the Single Currency. So that is what they will get. On both issues I am now firmly persuaded that it might be a good idea to have one. But I am equally firmly persuaded that it might not be a good idea. And you can't get much firmer than that! So much for those who say that I am not firm. This is my new policy and I expect everyone in the party to get firmly behind me.

Thursday

My speech was another triumph. My new firm policy resulted in a huge victory of 5 votes in the big European debate. Only one Conservative voted against me, i.e. my very ex-friend Norma Lamont. He told the TV cameras outside the Houses of Parliament that he was only against me because I had not made my position clear. What nonsense. I had made it perfectly clear that I was both for and against. You can't get much clearer than that! Obviously he must have been to visit his friend Mr Onanugu at Thresher's before the debate. All I can say is that it is a great shame Ryman's has collapsed, otherwise I would have gone out to buy a special new book to be called "The Biggest Bastard Of Them All Book", which would have just one name in it, written on every page in different coloured biros, depending on my mood and availability from Ryman's.

Friday

At 6 o'clock this morning I was considerably woken up by

my brother Terry, who was ringing from Gatwick to say he was just off to Ireland for his holiday. What he wanted to know was if he could get me another Aran Island pullover, like the one I left behind once at Mrs Kierans', when I had to come to rescue Cyril the Squirrel, who wouldn't come out from behind the sink.

BY ROYAL
DISAPPOINTMENT

I was in no small measure very angry with him for going off to Ireland without asking me. "Don't you realise," I said, "that, thanks to my historic Framework Document, there is now peace in Ireland. Therefore it would be very dangerous for you to go there. You are a top-security risk, due to your high-profile position." Terry thought for a moment and said: "John, just for once, you are right. As a famous author and celebrity I might easily be a target. I will go to Birmingham instead. The NEC is holding a very interesting exhibition about caravans called 'International Mobile Home '95'. "

Saturday

Poor Mr Clarke has put his foot in it. This is very unfortunate. It would be in no small measure unfair to dwell on the details of his gaffe but for the record Mr Clarke said there was a thriving steelworks at a place called Consett. And there isn't. We closed it down ages ago, which he should have known. I feel very sorry for him. Mr Clarke can never be Prime Minister now. No one who makes those sort of mistakes will ever be forgiven by the public. I said this to Terry, who rang from a Chevrolet Supertraveller at the NEC. "You're right," he said. "You and Norman should move into one of these and go camping."

Of course, if you are someone like Terry, such mistakes do not matter so much, e.g. the name of my cricket bat was not an Arnold Sutton but a J.B. Croydon (see page 378 of his so-called book). On second thoughts, maybe Terry should be Chancellor of the Exchequer!

Sunday

My wife Norman tells me that we are getting rid of the Constable in No. 10. "But I like him," I said. "He is very friendly and helps Mr Hanley with the crossword when I am too busy." "No," she said. "Constable is a painter."

"But we've just had the place redecorated," I said. It is typical of women that they always want to change everything.

Monday

I am in no small measure not inconsiderably very angry with Mr Clinton. He has spoilt my Irish peace process by agreeing to be photographed with Mr Adams at the White House. This has made me very, very cross indeed. Does Mr Clinton not realise that Mr Adams is a terrorist?

Mr Hurd then told me that he had arranged a historic trip for me to Israel to meet somebody called Mr Arafat. "Who is he?" I asked. "Let us just say," said Mr Hurd, "that it will do you a lot of good to be photographed with him."

Fair enough, but in the meantime I decided to send Mr Clinton a very tough letter, telling him exactly what I think of him.

This is how it went:

Dear Mr Clinton,

You probably don't remember me, but I have a special relationship with you. Oh yes! Anyway, how are you? I am fine. My wife Norman sends her regards to your wife Mrs Clinton.

Yours sincerely,
John Major

P.S. I think you should know that Mr Adams is a terrorist, and it would be a very bad idea for you to meet him.
P.P.S. If you meet him I will put you in one of my books.

Tuesday

Today I arrived in a place called Gaza Strip. It is very hot. Apparently I am the first world leader to come here since Mr Arafat took over, apart from the prime minister of Iceland and the foreign minister of Mauritius. Mr Arafat met me at the airport and we drove round his new country.

When we had finished five minutes later we went back to the hotel, where the receptionist said that there was a phone call for "a Mr Major". Was there anyone of that name with my party? "Who is it?" I asked. "It is the President of the United States of America," she replied. "Tell him I am in a meeting,"

I said firmly, just like Mr Clarke does when I ring him up. That will show Mr Clinton just how annoyed I am with him for meddling in the affairs of countries he knows nothing about.

Wednesday

Today I gave Mr Arafat a present as a gesture of goodwill for his peacemaking efforts. It was six armoured cars, which he can use to round up all his opponents in the new Palestinian democracy. In exchange he gave me a tea towel, which Norman was very pleased with. She told him that it was just what we wanted, as the one with daffodils on that we had bought in the Lake District had got a burn mark on it when I used it to take a portion of oven-ready chips out of the cooker. While we were exchanging our gifts a mobile phone rang on the belt of one of Mr Arafat's bodyguards. It was Mr Clinton trying to get in touch with me. "I know he is with you," said the President to Mr Arafat, "because I have just seen him on our satellite." I waved the phone away with a very statesmanlike gesture. "Tell him I am still in a meeting," I said. Mr Arafat then asked if I needed his help as peacemaker.

Thursday

At 2 o'clock this morning I was woken up by the phone ringing in our hotel room. It was Mr Clinton. "I am sorry," I said, "I cannot talk to you because I am asleep," and put the phone down. In fact I was not asleep, because his call had woken me up, but I was not going to tell him that.

A few minutes later the phone rang again. This time it was my brother Terry. He said: "Bill Clinton's been trying to get hold of you, John. Where have you been? He said you were asleep, but you sound pretty awake to me." "It is of no concern of yours whether I am awake or asleep," I said, in the voice I use to call Mr Blair a dimwit in the House of Commons. "Kindly keep your nose out of world affairs. You should stick to something you are good at like writing books.

Not that you are any good at that either, since they are full of mistakes, like saying that I fell off the donkey when we were at Margate. It wasn't Margate, it was Ramsgate. And it wasn't a donkey, it was my bike." "That's OK, John," he said, "I'll correct it in the paperback edition, which incidentally is coming out next week, 100,000 print run. Oh, and I promised my new friend Bill that he would get an autographed copy thanking him for his great work for peace in Northern Ireland." At this point I hung up and told the hotel switchboard that they were to put no more calls through to our room, particularly if they were from the President of the United States or my brother Terry.

Friday

When I arrived home I was very surprised to see a placard at the airport saying "'Economy No Good' Says Clarke". When I left three days ago everything had been fine.

When I got back to Number 10 I immediately rang up Mr Clarke to ask what on earth he meant. His secretary sounded very embarrassed and said that he could not speak to me because he was in a meeting. "Ask him to ring me very urgently," I said. Then my telephone rang. It was Mr Clinton. "I'm sorry," I said. "I cannot speak to you. I am talking to someone who is in a meeting."

I waited several hours for Mr Clarke to ring me back, and eventually I received a fax from his assistant. "It's very simple," it read. "We talk down the economy now, and then later whoever is prime minister can tell the country that everything's coming up roses. Neat, eh?"

Saturday

Mr Clarke has made another very stupid gaffe. He said there was a disposable nappy factory in a place called Consett which is in the North of England when there isn't because it was closed down.

"Nappies are not the only things that are disposable," I told Mr Clarke, when he finally answered my call. "You are right, John," he said with a laugh.

Sunday

Good news! Mr Clarke has not made a gaffe today (so far at least). Clearly my talking-to has had some effect. Oh yes.

After lunch the phone rang again. Norman answered it and said "Yes he is here," before I could say that I wasn't.

It was Mr Clinton who said he was doing everything to

persuade the IRA to give up their arms. "That is my job," I said. "And anyway you are only using the whole Irish question to boost your sagging popularity."

"So tell me all about it, buddy," he said in what I considered to be in no small measure a flippant manner. He then told me to "get a life" and rang off.

April

Monday

This is a very historic day. Apparently we are about to go to war over some fish. I was told this on the telephone this morning by Sir Leon Brittain. "Quite right," I said, "we must defend the rights of our fishermen against the Spanish." "No," he said. "We are defending the rights of the Spanish against the Canadians. I want you to put the entire Royal Navy on immediate battle alert to support our Spanish partners against the infamous pirates of the Royal Canadian Fisheries Patrol Inspectorate." After he had rung off with the words "That is an order," I called in Mr Hurd to explain to me what was going on. "It is very complicated, prime minister," he said. "It is very important for us to steer a middle path on this one. On the one hand, the Spanish are totally in the wrong. But on the other, the Canadians are totally in the right. So you can see that it would be quite inappropriate for us to do anything at all." "So we are caught in the middle?" I said. "Yes," he said, "like the fish." I thought this was a typical Foreign Office joke, so I ignored it, and asked him if nothing could be done. "Exactly, prime minister," he said.

Tuesday

Today is another very historic day. I have decided to give an exclusive interview to the *Daily Telegraph*. They rang up at half-past three saying that they needed something for page 13 because their interview with someone called Liz Hurley had fallen through. When their reporter arrived I made a number of important points:

1. I am not going to resign.
2. I am staying.
3. Oh yes.

"But surely," said the reporter, rather rudely in my judgement, "everyone is agreed that the man at the top should go?" "You are quite right," I said. "Mr Hanley must resign at once." When I had thought about it, I realised what a very sound decision this was. After all, I had only given him the job in the first place because I had enjoyed his mother's performance in the film *Genevieve*, and because he had once bought me a cake in the House of Commons tea room. I now realise that these are insufficient grounds for making someone Chairman of the Conservative party.

Wednesday

I am not sure that I have taken the right decision about Mr Hanley. Not that I have taken a decision yet, oh no. He has many good points. Only this morning he asked me whether I could help him with 27 down — "scaly creature that swims in the sea", four letters beginning with "F". "Frog," I said, quick as a flash. "Brilliant, prime minister," he said. "I was just going to put in 'fish'." Mr Hanley is a very nice man, and I should be very sorry to see him go, if I sacked him, which I probably will not. On the other hand, we are looking for someone to blame when we lose the council elections, which of course we won't, and he might well be a suitable candidate.

Thursday

I have had a brilliant idea, which Mr Aitken suggested to me this morning on his way to Iran with a large suitcase marked "Guns". We are not going to blame Mr Hanley, after all. We are going to blame the BBC. It is all the fault of people like Mr Humphrys who ask rude questions on the *Today* progamme, which I do not listen to anyway, because my wife Norman has our bedside radio tuned to Classic FM for the Operatic Highlights slot. Anyway, blaming the BBC is bound to be very popular.

Friday

All the newspapers have got it wrong again, as usual. The *Daily Telegraph* this morning said: "Pathetic Major Lashes Out At BBC In Desperate Attempt To Divert Attraction From His Abysmal Failures. More pics of Liz

Hurley pages 8, 9, 10 and 12." Fortunately the BBC must feel very guilty about this, because they rang up to ask whether I would come on *Panorama* to do a very important 40-minute interview in time for the local elections. Mr Hanley advised against this, saying it would not do us any good. Talk about being ungrateful. Perhaps I  will have to sack him after all, and then he will have to do his own crossword clues.

Saturday

Today is a very historic day, as it is the Boat Race. My money is on either Oxford or Cambridge. My brother Terry rang up to say that he had been asked to do a special guest commentary on Radio Mortlake FM. "I am not interested," I said. "I am going on *Panorama*, which is much more important." "Well you might be interested in this," he said. "I have just been to the International Gnome Conference and have been approached by a very important antique dealer, who says that he has a garden gnome made by you personally, and that it is worth a great deal of money." "How can he possibly know it was one of mine?" I said. "Because," he replied, "it has the wrong hat, yellow instead of green, which is a mistake you were always making, because you had your mind on Mrs Kierans down the road."

Sunday

My friend Mr Aitken has been attacked by the newspapers for selling weapons to Iran, although he did not know about it. This is no reason for him to resign. After all, we were selling arms to Iraq, so he was just helping to even things out a bit. I rang him and told him that he had my full support. For some reason he began crying and shouting, "No, please!" He is obviously having a breakdown and I may have to sack him after all. Talking of sacking people, Mr Hanley has announced that there will be tax cuts to pay for the cost of the break up of the NHS, the education system and the welfare services.

This is in no small measure annoying of Mr Hanley since having tax cuts is my brilliant idea for winning the next election.

I made a speech about it in a place called Birmingham which is in the middle of England which is highly appropriate since I have decided to capture Middle England. Oh yes. As I said: "I am going to drive in the middle lane of the middle of the road, in the middle of the night, straight to Middle England."

This is my new metaphor. And I will not allow Mr Blair to come up behind me flashing his lights and force me on to the hard shoulder where I will break down and have to wait by my car for the AA men to come. Oh no!

My speech must have been a great success because when I asked the chairman what he thought he said it was "middling, to say the least". This shows my message is already catching on.

Monday

Today I flew in Concorde to America and my wife Norman asked me: "Where is this Middle England that you keep talking about?"

"It is down there," I said, pointing to a green patch you could see through the clouds.

"It is very small," she said.

"Yes," I agreed. "There will not be room there for both me and Mr Blair."

"Oh dear," she said with a funny smile which was very irritating, nearly as irritating as the complimentary packet of salted peanuts which I could not open to have with my refreshing fruit beverage, which incidentally I spilled over my trousers during some turbulence. Luckily Norman still had her hot towel to mop it up, even though it was cold by then.

Tuesday

My trip to America has been acclaimed as a not unhistoric success. Mr Clinton remembered at once who I was and listened very carefully while I explained why he was wrong about Ireland. Then he said: "That's very interesting, John, but it is time for my saxophone practice. Have a nice day."

Showing me out, one of Mr Clinton's aides told me that "The President must think a lot of you, bud. You got a whole two minutes." I asked him how long Mr Adams had got and he said "Only 12 hours", and gave me a baseball cap saying "Vote Clinton!" This shows the special relationship is very much alive indeed. Oh yes!

Back home I am in no small measure annoyed with the BBC for not showing my brilliant *Panorama* interview with Mr Dimbleby. They say that they were told not to broadcast it by a Judge in Scotland on the grounds that it would prejudice the result of the Scottish elections.

"That is ridiculous," said Mr Hanley. "No one would vote for you after seeing it."

Perhaps Mr Hanley will have to look for a new job in the summer after all.

Wednesday

As it happens, Mr Hanley was wrong. We have lost all our seats in Scotland, even though the broadcast did not go out. He really is hopeless. He went on the radio to say that the result was a typical mid-term hiccup. I was not convinced at all.

A lot of people are now saying that it is time for me to go. Well I have got news for them. I am going. Oh yes. I am going to stay.

(This joke was written for me by Mr Morris Norris who helps me with my off-the-cuff remarks.)

Anyway who could possibly replace me as leader? I have drawn up a list of so-called stalking horses, just like they do with the Grand National and have written their "form" beside the names.

THE LIST

Mr Clarke. Hopeless. Too many gaffes.

Mr Hurd. Hopeless. And too old.

Mr Heseltine. Hopeless. And has a bad heart.

Mr Portillo. Hopeless. And too clever.

Mrs Bottomley. Hopeless. She will have to go.

I read them out to my wife Norman over our new breakfast cereal which we had bought in an American supermarket. It is called Pablo's Original Tortilla Chips and it tastes rather odd with milk. I asked Norman whether she thought I had left anyone hopeless off the list. She gave me a funny look and said: "What about the favourite?"

Thursday

My friend Mr Aitken has been in the newspapers again, in a lot of stories about him and various Arabs. The headlines all say that he should resign which is an improvement on them saying that I should resign.

In fact I was so grateful to Mr Aitken for this that I agreed to let him use my autocue for his impromptu denial of the stories and his announcement of a great crusade against the press.

"I am going to sue the lot of them, prime minister," he told me.

"But how can you afford to sue everyone?" I asked him. "Since litigation is so expensive — as I know from my own experience when they said I had not had an affair with the cook."

"Money is no object," said Mr Aitken. "I've made so much from these Arabs over the years that I won't even notice it. Even if I lose, which I probably will."

Friday

Mr Aitken has not acted a minute too soon in my judgement. Another member of my government has been exposed by the newspapers. It is a Mr Spring who I had not heard of until he wrote to me and resigned.

Anyway, the press invaded his privacy and scandalously revealed that he spends his Sunday evenings innocently going to bed with a friend of his and the friend's girlfriend. This is appalling.

Mr Hanley agreed. "This is appalling," he said, showing me the *News of the World*. "Listen to what he says about your wife." Then he read it out to me.

"Norman is a little cracker but the poor thing only gets it once a year from her husband because he's such a wimp." I thanked Mr Hanley for his kindness in pointing this out and then made a decisive decision as I always do.

"Mr Spring must resign immediately. Thank goodness the newspapers have got their eye on people like that."

When I went home upstairs I found my brother Terry had

let himself in and was busy talking to Norman.

"Is it really once a year?" he said. "It wasn't like that with Mrs Kierans. Though of course I did not put that in my book out of respect for him."

I was in no mood whatsoever to listen to my brother's reminiscences. "If I wanted some smut," I told him in my stern telling-Mr-Blair-off voice, "I would watch *Blind Date*."

"Perhaps you should go on it," said Norman, rather missing the point as usual.

Saturday

A very quiet weekend. No one resigned at all and there was no sleaze anywhere. Mr Aitken's sword and shield are obviously doing a good job in cleaning up the cancer of irresponsible newspapers.

Sunday

Thank goodness for the *Sunday Times*, who attacked Labour's Mr Prescott who is clearly up to his neck in corruption. Apparently someone bought him a drink in a pub in 1973 and he did not declare it in the Members' Interests Book.

This shows at last what we Conservatives have known all along. It is the *Labour* party which is the party of sleaze and is not fit to govern as long as I am Prime Minister. Which I am. Oh yes.

Monday

Our friends in the press have scored another triumph for truth and fair play by attacking Mr Blunkett and his dog. Under the headline "Blind Drunk with Power," the *Daily Mail* revealed just what Blunkett would do to the teachers if Labour were ever let into power — i.e. sack them and close down the bad schools.

Everybody knows this is our idea and the Labour Party are so sleazy and corrupt that all they can do is steal ideas from us.

Mr Blair is even trying to steal my job. But I am here to stay, as I told my wife Norman.

"Oh yes," I said.

"Oh no!" she replied.

"We are not in a pantomime," I told her.

"You could have fooled me," she replied.

May

Tuesday

Today is even more historic than a number of other days I have called historic. By a brilliant move, which not even Mr Hurd could have thought of, I have put down the rebellion over Europe. I rang up Mrs Gorman and told her that she and her friends were now members of the Conservative Party again. "What's the catch?" she said, "What do we have to do?" "You have to vote for me on all occasions," I said. "No way," she said in an angry voice. "Alright," I said. "It's a deal."

I then pulled out my "Bastards" book and crossed out all the names in a special red biro. Except Sir Richard Body who is not in the "Bastards" book because he has a special book all of his own, called "Loonies". So ends the sorry tale of the so-called "Euro-rebels".

Wednesday

The rebels are in all the newspapers saying that they are going to go on voting against me if they feel like it. I was very angry about this, as I immediately had to write all their names out again in the "Bastards" book, this time in green ink, which took a not inconsiderable amount of my valuable time. However Mr Hanley came in to say that it was good news about the rebels, because we could still blame them when we lose the council elections next week. "But we are not going to lose the elections," I said. "I saw a programme on the television last night which said we were going to do very well." "That was our party political broadcast you idiot, I mean prime minister" he said.

Meanwhile I was in no small measure very considerably annoyed when I read in the *Telegraph* this morning that the woman I do not mention, i.e. Mrs Thatcher, has been given the Garter by Her Majesty the Queen. "What has Mrs Thatcher ever done to deserve this?" I asked my wife Norman over our plate of McAlpen muesli-style cereal. "Well, she made you prime minister," said Norman, "even if she now realises that it was a mistake." I did not have time to argue with her about Mrs Thatcher, whose views do not bother me in the slightest, as I had to get down to Ryman's to buy a new book called "Royal Bastards" to put the Queen in.

Talking of Mrs Thatcher, which I never do, Mr Blair has again made a complete fool of himself by saying that he admired her. When I told the Cabinet about it, Mr Portaloo muttered very loudly under his breath "Well we all know why Mr Blair admires Mrs Thatcher. Because she chose a successor he would find it so easy to beat". "I heard that," I said sternly. "You were meant to," replied Mr Portaloo.

Thursday

My brother Terry rang me at 3 o'clock this morning to say that he was in New Zealand. "You ought to be out here, John," he said, "I am the guest of honour at the Waitangi Ideal Gnome Exhibition, the biggest show of gardening ornaments ever held in the Southern Hemisphere." "Is that all you have woken me up to say?" I said. "No," said Terry, "I wanted to tell you that gnome technology is in a different universe since our day. There are these new electronic gnomes from Korea which walk around the garden singing 'Hi ho, Hi ho'. Can you imagine trying to make one of those, when you couldn't even make a cement one without getting the colour of the hat wrong." As a world leader I was not prepared to be spoken to like that by my brother in the middle of the night so I hung up.

No sooner had I got back to sleep, dreaming of the woman I never dream of being strangled with a garter, when the phone rang again. It was Terry saying he had been cut off, just as he was about to tell me about an interview he had given to the *Wellington Herald* about his memories of VE-Day. "You mustn't miss it," he said, "I've told the story of how you were asleep in your cot when Mr Churchill announced that we had won the war, and father rushed out to make a special Victory Gnome with two fingers raised." "I am not asleep now," I told him, "and I have got two fingers raised". "Why?" asked Terry, "when you are just about to *lose* the local elections."

Friday

Today I won yet another historic victory over Mr Blair at Question Time. He made a very silly joke about the Euro-rebels, saying that I had surrendered to them

and that whereas he led his party, I only followed mine. This was so pathetic that everyone laughed at him. I immediately came back with the brilliant reply, "You are the one who has surrendered, i.e. to the men in Brussels. You are the one who has put up the white flag in the fast lane rather than driving carefully in the slow lane with a red flag in front of us to let everyone know we are coming. Oh yes." This very clever ad-lib completely silenced everyone.

Saturday

I have had an absolutely brilliant idea for celebrating VE-Day, which I read about in Mr Hanley's *Daily Mirror*, which he now gets to do the crossword because he says the *Telegraph* one is too difficult. We are going to have a special two minutes silence, even in the House of Commons. "I myself will say nothing," I told Mr Hanley. "So what's new?" he asked, totally missing the point that this is a new idea which I have thought up, and which could easily win us next week's local elections.

Monday

I have had another brilliant idea to win the local elections. We are going to solve the problems of the inner cities. The way I am going to do it is to be photographed in front of some tower blocks.

"Just like Mrs Thatcher," said Mr Hanley, rather stupidly. "Not at all," I told him in no uncertain terms. "Unlike Mrs Thatcher, I actually put up the tower blocks in the first place."

"This is a grey, soulless wasteland," I told the newspapers, "and all the fault of the Labour councils. Except for the ones that were the fault of the Tory councils." Let Mr Blair try and wriggle out of that one!

Tuesday

I have had enough of Mr Blair. I am going to call Mr Blair's ideas "Soap powder politics dissolved in sound-bites".

"This will go down well with the punters and will get you on the Nine O'Clock News," said my speechwriter Mr Morris Norris, who wrote it for me.

Sure enough, there I was on South-East News, just after the tree protesters and before the traffic update.

I am now confident that I will win the Local Elections. In 50 years' time, this will be known as "L.E. Day". Oh yes.

"It will be a historic landslide," I told my wife Norman. "And you will be at the bottom of it," she replied, showing that she is at last understanding my job.

Friday

We have not done anything like as badly in the local elections as some people said we would, i.e. Mr Hanley. He said it would be a disaster if we lost 2,000 seats, and in fact we only lost 2,200, so it was not a disaster at all. So much for Mr Hanley. I asked Mr Morris Norris to write me out an upbeat speech explaining why this showed that we were going to win the next general election. He gave me a funny look and asked if he could be sacked instead. In the end I wrote my own speech which I think not even Mr Churchill could have improved on. Oh no. It went in no small measure like this. "When the British people have got their backs to the wall, like in the war, they turn round and fight." When I read out my speech to Mr Hurd he said in his typically toffee-nosed way, "I think our problem, prime minister, is that it is you who have got your back to the wall while the British people are against you." "But I will still turn round and fight," I said in my new "bulldog" voice. "Forgive me, prime minister, but to elaborate on your metaphor, if you turn round when you have your back to the wall, that means you are now *facing* the wall, rather like the dunce in a school classroom." He then gave me one of his silly little upper-class sniggers and said that he would love to hear more of my speech but that he was sure I was far too busy.

Saturday

Today is a very historic day indeed, as I am the first British prime minister to go to Northern Ireland since Mrs Thatcher. I was able to do this only because my peace process has been such a complete triumph and now the violence is completely ended. When I arrived in a place called Londonderry (which is not in London at all, but in Derry) everybody was so excited to see me that they started throwing stones at the police. My friend Sir Patrick Mayhew explained that this was a traditional Irish way of welcoming visitors.

Sunday

My press man Mr Meyer has told me that it is very important for me to go abroad for the great VE-Day celebrations. This way I can be seen on television as a world leader with all the other world leaders, which I am. Oh yes. Today I had to go to Paris in France where we saw thousands of French soldiers marching down the Champs Elysees. It was very impressive and I asked Mr Meyer why we hadn't had any troops marching down the streets of London. "That would have been difficult, prime minister," he explained, "since you asked Mr Rifkind to abolish most of the army to pay for your tax cuts." I ignored this unhelpful remark and prepared for my historic conversations with Mr Herr Kohl and Mr Monsieur Chirac, who has just been elected as the new President of France. I was particularly encouraged by this as Mr Monsieur Chirac is a Conservative. I was going to tell him that this was a very good omen for me, but unfortunately I could not because of a mistake in the seating plan. I could see Mr Herr Kohl and Mr Monsieur Chirac sitting together on the big table, but I was sitting at a small table near the kitchen with a Mr Chief Awolowu from the Cameroons. He told me how much he admired our British prime minister Mrs Thatcher. This made me even more annoyed than I had been by the silly mistake in the seating plan.

Monday

It is not only the French who make mistakes in the seating plan, as I discovered today in Moscow which is in Russia. I was there to watch lots of Russian troops marching through Red Square to celebrate their victory over Chechnya. I was really looking forward to talking to Mr Yeltsin

and my special friend
Mr Clinton, but
unfortunately when we
had lunch I found that
they were on the big
table, and I was on a
small table by the toilet
with a Mr President
Nazhikahmed from
Uzbekistan. He told me
how much he admired
our British prime

minister Mrs Thatcher. I am looking forward to getting back
to a country where I am appreciated!

Tuesday

When I got home I was very encouraged to see Mr
Heseltine on the television rallying all Conservatives to
support me. Not that they don't already. Oh no. But it was
still very kind of him to say "We Tories must stop criticising
John Major. We must stop going on about his failures and the
need to replace him with an older more vigorous man who
can unite the party." This is just the kind of support I need. It
is good to know that at least one Conservative is still loyal.

Wednesday

Mrs Bottomley is very unpopular because she has decided
to close all the hospitals in London. In our Cabinet meeting
she told us that there could be "no U-turn on this issue".

This is not true because as soon as she left the room we all
decided that we would stop supporting her as soon as we had
voted for her silly plan.

In the Commons we all sat as far away from her as we
could so that the camera would make it look as if she was all
on her own. This will be good practice for her because after
the reshuffle (which will make me popular again) she will be
very considerably on her own at home. Oh yes!

Thursday

Mr Nolan has sent me his report which is very good
indeed. It has a new code of conduct in it which is rather like
one of my charters. The main points are that MPs should not:

1). Lie
2). Cheat
3). Steal

This is radical stuff but I think I can persuade most of the party to go along with it (though I am not sure about Mr Aitken).

Friday

Mr Nolan's report is actually very bad indeed. Mr Hanley has now read all of it and has told me that Mr Nolan wants to know where the Tory Party gets all its funds from. How dare he! Who does he think he is? Who appointed Mr Nolan anyway? He should mind his own business.

When I asked Mr Hanley where we *do* get the money from he went red and said that a lot of it came from people who lie, cheat and steal.

"But they are not politicians, are they?" I said. "So that is all right."

"Mr Nolan has a lot to learn about politics," I said later to my wife Norman over our late-night half-past-nine drinks of Ovaltine.

"And you should know," she said supportively.

June

Sunday

I am in my judgement beside myself with rage at Mrs Thatcher's latest attempt to attack me. "It is like the film about the shark," said my wife Norman. "Just when you think it is safe to go into the water, she appears again with her big teeth, saying you're no good." "It is not at all like that," I replied in my special angry-with-Mr-Hanley voice. "For a start, I am not at all frightened of her. And secondly, she comes out of the water and writes articles in the *Sunday Times*, which the shark never did." "You're right," said Norman. "The comparison doesn't work, because in the film everyone doesn't prefer the shark to the lifeguard."

"I have better things to do," I told her, "than to sit around here discussing sharks." I have decided to take absolutely no notice of anything Mrs Jaws says, and I have told Mr Meyer to brief all the press to this effect."

Monday

I have stayed up nearly all the night writing down all the reasons why Mrs Thatcher is wrong about me, in a new book from Ryman's, which I have codenamed "Mrs Shark". She says:

1. I am weak over Europe. NOT TRUE. We stood up to them over Maastricht and only agreed to do what they had wanted at the last minute. Also, Mr Hurd and I threw out the Belgian federalist M. Dehaene for President, and it was entirely due to us that we got Mr Santer instead, who is a federalist from Luxembourg.

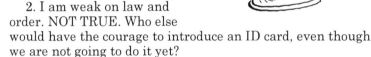

2. I am weak on law and order. NOT TRUE. Who else would have the courage to introduce an ID card, even though we are not going to do it yet?

3. All my other policies are pathetic too. NOT TRUE. If they are so pathetic, why has Mr Blair tried to copy them all? No one says he's pathetic.

Anyway, enough of Mrs Thatcher. I am not going to waste any more time on showing how everything she says in the *Sunday Times* is wrong.

Tuesday

Who does Mrs Thatcher think took us into the disaster of the ERM? It was her, that's who. When Mr Hurd and the then-Chancellor (me) went to tell her that Britain should join, she pathetically gave in. She should have stood up to us, just like I stood up to Mr Herr Kohl and all the others.

Talking of which, I today had a historic call from the new President of France, Mr Monsieur Chirac, who has just been staying with Mr Herr Kohl for a summit conference. He of course wanted to involve me in their top-level discussions. This is how it went:

Chirac: Bonjour, M. Major. Avez-vous lu le *Sunday Times*? Magnifique, non? Quelle dame!

Me: Oh, hullo, Mr President.

Chirac: Herr Kohl et moi, nous avons decidés tous. Comprenez?

Me: Thank you very much for ringing.

Chirac: Ha, ha, ha. Quelle dame...

I think this conversation shows that I am still very much at the heart of Europe. Even if we are going slowly in the fast lane, due to fog, which is after all only prudent in the circumstances.

Wednesday

No one is talking about Mrs Thatcher any more, which is a relief. They are all talking about Mr Lord Nolan, who is the man I appointed last year to stop people talking about sleaze. Mr Lord Nolan has got it wrong when he says that we should introduce new measures to stop MPs cashing in on their position. Firstly people do not go into politics simply to cash in. And secondly, if these kind of measures are introduced, no one will want to go into politics because they cannot cash in. In my judgement, it is most important that the House of Commons should include MPs from the widest range of walks of life — e.g. consultants, management advisers, public relations experts and so forth.

Thursday

The Thatcher affair is now entirely forgotten, though it is very interesting that the one thing Mrs Thatcher does not mention in her list of why my government is so hopeless is Northern Ireland. It is not surprising since I am the one who brought peace to the provinces and she did not. However, I have no intention of using this very good point against her, because I am not in the least interested in Mrs Thatcher and her new book *Jaws II*. Oh no.

Incidentally we have just lost another by-election in Scotland but it is not a historic day by any manner of means.

"We may have lost the seat," as Mr Hanley said on the Classic-FM News, "but Mr Blair failed to win it."

This obviously makes it a disaster for Mr Blair rather than us. It is good to see that sometimes Mr Hanley still talks sense!

Friday

Mr Blair has a silly new idea to get more women into politics. He obviously has no idea what this can lead to (see above).

Saturday

Mrs Thatcher has now announced that she admires Mr Blair. This shows how out of touch she is with the country. After complaining about how disloyal everyone was to her, she has proved that she is more disloyal than everyone put together. And I shall say so. Oh yes.

I said to Mr Hanley: "She is asking people to vote Labour." "I wouldn't worry about it," he told me. "They are going to do that anyway."

Sunday

I have had to make a very important decision about Bosnia, which is in Yugoslavia. The Serbians (the ones in Bosnia) have kidnapped 30 British soldiers, which is nearly the whole British Army.

"They must not get away with this," I said to Mr Hurd. "What shall I do?"

Mr Hurd replied: "You do nothing, prime minister. I will immediately send out more troops."

"And what will they do?" I asked authoritatively.

"They will withdraw at once along with all the others. This will show the Serbs that we mean business."

As I said to Norman over our breakfast of sauerkraut (which Mr Herr Kohl had given to me in a big jar as a symbol of our special friendship): "I am sending in the troops. This is my Falklands."

"Yes," she said. "Except that we won the Falklands."

Once again Norman has missed the point, just like another woman who I could mention but never do.

Monday

I have discovered why there is no feelgood factor. It is nothing to do with me, as everyone seems to think. It is because of something called "negative equity", which means that your house is worth less than when you bought it, but you are still having to pay out hundreds of pounds a month for it, which means that you do not feel good. Oh no. I also know exactly who is to blame for negative equity — i.e. Mrs Thatcher, for encouraging people to buy houses. "But surely," said my wife Norman, "you were in Mrs Thatcher's government?" This silly remark only went to show that she has no idea of how the political process really works.

Tuesday

It is quite unbelievable. Mr Lord Justice Scott, who I appointed to find out who was to blame for the scandal over selling arms to Iraq, has apparently produced some kind of report listing the people who are to blame. How dare he, after all I have done for him, giving him a job and making him famous? No one would have heard of him if it wasn't for me. He is just like my brother Terry. Obviously Mr Lord Scott has no idea how politics really works. Apparently he has criticised my friend Mr Waldegrave for telling lies to the House of Commons. In fact, Mr Waldegrave was so upset that he immediately rang me up to ask me whether he had my full support. "Yes," I lied, showing that he is not the only one who can tell lies, just because he has been to Eton. I will decide whether to support him or not when I have read what the newspapers think I should do.

Wednesday

On further reading of the newspapers, I think I may after all have misjudged Mr Lord Scott. From the bits of his report which I have seen in the *Daily Mail*, he apparently thinks that I was in no way to blame. This shows that after all he has a very sound grasp of the way politics works. I read out the relevant passage to Norman over our new Euro-regulation croissants (which are square). He said: "I conclude that, as Foreign Secretary, Mr Major had no idea what was going on." "So what's new?" said Norman, for once taking a supportive line, which was extremely welcome.

Thursday

I was in no small measure very irritated indeed when my brother Terry rang up early in the morning to say that he was going to be on a very important TV programme about the week's news called *Have I Got News For You*. "What are the big stories this week, John?" he asked. "I have been too busy being a celebrity to read the papers. Have you done anything I should know about?" "Yes," I said to him, wanting to show that I know just as many famous people as he does. "I have been to a party and met a very famous writer called Eve Pollard, who has been on TV even more times than you." "Oh," he laughed, "you didn't go to *that*, did you? We were all invited to that, but it was the same night as John Paul Getty's dance, which was much more 'A' List. Anyway, make sure you tune in tomorrow night at ten — I am thinking up some very funny jokes about you! I will not mention Mrs Kierans, I promise — oh no, as you would say, ha, ha, ha!" "I have better things to do than watch you on silly television shows," I told him in my "I've-got-a-country-to-run" voice. "Get real," he said and rang off.

Friday

I have to say that if there is one person in the world even more irritating than my brother Terry it is my ex-friend Mr Lamont. He has been on the *Today* programme saying that I should make my mind up about the Single Currency. This just goes to show that he doesn't know how politics works. I have said it before and I shall say it again. I have made up my mind about the Single Currency. I long ago decided that we would wait and see what happened. And then when the time comes, we may join, or we may not. There are even rumours that Mr Lamont wants to be prime minister, which is ridiculous. How could anyone who was a complete failure as Chancellor become prime minister?

Saturday

Today I got on a plane and flew to the heart of Europe where I met Mr Monsieur Chirac who has taken over from Mr Monsieur Mitterrand as President of France. To my surprise I found that he is in full agreement with me about Europe. I think Britain should not join in the Common Currency and he thinks Britain should leave the EC entirely!

"We speak the same language," I said, "except you speak French and I speak English."

"Vous êtes un idiot," he replied, which Mr Hurd tells me is a rarely used term of respect between two great statesmen.

Sunday

Mr Portaloo has made a fool of himself by saying that he is against a single European currency. He told the reporters that all the talk of fast lanes, slow lanes and emergency flashing lights on the hard shoulder was "rubbish".

Obviously he has no grasp of politics because he does not know that it was me who invented these ideas!

In my view Mr Portaloo is only fit to sit in the Little Chef service station as we drive past hooting and jeering on our way to the slip-road which takes us onto the roundabout near the flyover leading to the middle lane to Europe with the contraflow system and the cones!

That is my vision. Oh yes!

Thursday

Today I bought a new book at Ryman's to put in the names of all the people who must not get my job. The first name is obviously Mrs Thatcher who has been on television wearing a silly hat and being given some award by the Queen. She will clearly do anything to publicise her new book *Why I Hate John Major* (Collins £15.99) which I have no intention of reading, although I have marked certain passages in red biro which are not true, e.g. "I never thought Major was any good. It was not my idea to appoint him. I was forced into it by Nigel and Geoffrey." While my wife Norman and I were watching the ceremony on TV, I asked her whether she thought that the Queen would ever give me this honour. "I doubt it," she says, "unless they change its name to the Citizen's Garter."

While I am on the subject of honours, my new "Classless Honours List" is coming out tomorrow, chosen by the ordinary people of this country who have rung up the special "Honours Hotline" (0898-222-111, which is incidentally the same number as the Cones Hotline). I was very pleased to see that the pop star Cliff Richard has won a knighthood. "A brilliant move," said Mr Hanley, "this will really appeal to young voters. It could be the beginning of our recovery." Not of course that we need one, as we are doing very well and are only 58 points behind Mr Blair in the polls.

Friday

Today I put several more names in my book, including:

● Mr Heseltine, who was on the *Today* programme saying that he totally supported me and couldn't understand why the media were going on about a leadership crisis.

● Mr Portaloo, who was interviewed in the *Telegraph* saying that he totally supported me, and couldn't imagine why all the Tory MPs were going on about a leadership contest.

● Mr Lamont, who was apparently on the *Good Morning Kingston-upon-Thames Show*, saying that he could not understand why anyone supported me and that, if there was a leadership contest, he would be voting for the best man for the job — i.e. himself.

Monday

I'm afraid that a not inconsiderable number of new names will have to go into my book after the meeting I had with the new Euro-Sceptic party. These are the Conservative MPs who do not seem to know the meaning of the word loyalty. I went to see them to explain my very clear and firm policy on the Single European Currency, on which I have always been absolutely clearly and firm — i.e. that I have not yet made up my mind and I have absolutely no intention of doing so. Oh no. You can't get much clearer and firmer than that. But would you believe it, these ungrateful, disloyal and in no small measure totally rude MPs would not accept my very clear and firm view, and kept asking me to decide one way or the other. Eventually I did decide. Oh yes. I decided to leave the room. That showed them who was the leader of this party. All they could do was go off and give silly interviews to journalists about how they were going to elect a new leader. No wonder that we are doing so badly in the polls, not that we are, when I have so many MPs like this in my party. As I told Norman tonight over our usual late night, 9.30 cup of cheese-and-onion flavoured Horlicks, I sometimes think it would be better if I was the only Tory MP in the country. "Don't worry, dear," she said, "after the next election you will be." I went to sleep wondering whether I should put Norman's name in my new book.

Tuesday

I was very pleased to hear on the *Today* programme that I

have at least one friend. He is called Sir Patrick Mayhew who works in Northern Ireland. He has written a letter to the paper saying that unless everyone shuts up and rallies behind me, the IRA will start letting off bombs everywhere. That should stop all the talk of a leadership battle. Not that there is any.

I am not inconsiderably incandescent with rage at the behaviour of the Shell Oil company who have done something totally unforgivable — i.e. saying one minute that they will do something, and then the next, doing a complete U-turn and deciding to do the opposite. As I said to Norman: "These people are nothing but utter wimps." "Yes," she said thoughtfully, "and you should know."

Wednesday

Mr Justice Scott is certainly a man I will soon have to have a special book for. Yet again today there is another leak criticising Mr Waldegrave for having lied to the House of Commons. If Scott is going to make a fuss about little things like that, he will probably get upset at Mr Clark, Mr Rifkind and Mr Garel-Jones as well. All they did was try and put some men in prison. Honestly!

Mr Heseltine is telling everyone that he seems to be the only member of the government who will get off "Scott free", which I suppose is his clever way of saying he is going to be the next prime minister, which he is not going to be if I have anything to do with it. I have decided that when Mr Scott's report is published, which will be on Boxing Day when there are no papers, I will have to reject his findings. I cannot think whose idea it was to give him the job in the first place.

Thursday

Today is a very historic day. When Mr Hanley came in with his crossword, I told him that I had decided to resign as leader of the Tory party. But I shall stay on as Prime Minister.

It will be much easier to govern without the Conservative Party, as they have become very unpopular. This in my judgement is a very brilliant idea which will certainly put my name in the history books, as nobody has ever thought of it before. Mr Hanley asked me whether I could help him with 27 across, "giant Antipodean bird, 3 letters ending with U". "Lomu," I said, quick as a flash, to show that I have not lost touch with what is going on. Oh no.

Sunday

My historic idea has been a great success with the Cabinet. "We are all united now," said Mr Portaloo. "Everyone is delighted that you resigned." They all laughed good-naturedly. "You should have done it years ago," said Mr Heseltine. "We're all right behind you," said Mr Clarke. That is what loyalty is all about!

I then explained that there would have to be a contest for my job but only I would be standing so therefore I would win.

The Cabinet were all quite satisfied with this explanation. So much so that they all left in a hurry to go and pledge their loyalty to me from their various campaign headquarters.

Monday

I can't believe it! Mr Redwood is going to stand against me. I have put him in a new book called "The Double Bastard Book". Because that is what he is. Twice as much of a bastard as all the other bastards.

Mr Redwood has even been on television playing cricket. "He is trying to be like me," I said to my wife Norman. "Then he can't be very serious about winning," she replied as she wrapped the china in tissue paper and put it in the tea chest. Obviously to keep it safe from burglars.

Later on, my brother Terry rang to say that there would always be a job for me at his company. "Not as an electrician," he explained, "because you're not qualified, but I have a vacancy for a secretary to a high-flying media star who appears on radio and television and has had a successful book published and has even met Joan Collins."

Then he laughed and rang off.

July

Tuesday

Today is in my judgement the most historic day in the history of Britain. I have swept back to power with the biggest landslide victory that any prime minister has ever won. The historic moment came at precisely 5.22 p.m when Sir Marcus Fox rang up from the House of Commons and said: "Prime Minister, let me be the first to congratulate you. I am absolutely delighted to be able to tell you that the votes cast for each of the candidates were as follows:

"Sutch, Screaming Lord. Not standing.
"Redwood, Norman John Henry Vulcan. 89.
"Major (that is you, Prime Minister), John. 218.
"Papers spoiled by comments such as 'Bring back Thatch', 'They are both tossers' and 'Free Myra Hindley'. 18."

"So who has won then?" I asked Sir Marcus. "It is my humble duty to inform you, Prime Minister, that you are now the leader of the Conservative party and it is a tribute to your unique powers of leadership that only a tiny pathetic minority of 109 MPs were against you."

As soon as Sir Marcus had brought me this astonishing news, which was exactly what I had predicted, I went out into Downing Street to speak to the world's press, just like Mrs Thatcher used to do when we has retaken the Falkland Islands. This was the clear message I gave them:

1. The air is now completely cleared.
2. The boil is lanced.
3. We have now drawn a firm line under everything.
4. Let us now get on with the real job of this government which is to stop Mr Blair winning the next election.
5. This is a time for reconciliation and party unity.

A reporter from the *Newsnight* programme shouted out: "Does that mean you will be giving Mr Redwood his job back?" "Certainly not, he is a bastard," I replied in my new, no-nonsense, I-am-totally-in-charge-because-I-have-won-the-biggest-election-victory-in-history voice. Oh yes, make no mistake. I am the master now.

Wednesday

All night the messages of congratulations have been pouring in for my astonishing victory. Every single member of the Cabinet has written me a personal note saying that it is a tremendous personal tribute to my courage and leadership that I have won this overwhelming triumph, with only a third of the MPs against me. I have also had messages of support from all sorts of other people including Tory MPs, Party Chairmen and Terry's wife Shirley, who I have not spoken to since Christmas 1989. This shows that the whole country has rallied behind me, and that the boil is well and truly lanced.

Thursday

No sooner had my wife Norman taken my breakfast poached egg out of the microwave this morning, than there was a knock at the door. It was Mr Heseltine, who I had quite forgotten about in my hour of triumph. He was holding a crumpled piece of paper which he put on the table in front of me. "I expect you remember this," he said, with a curious smile. It read:

"I, John Major, hereby agree that in consideration for the agreement of Michael Roy Dibdin Heseltine not to stand against me in the leadership election, I will give the aforesaid M. Heseltine the following:

"1. That he shall enjoy the rank, title and position of Lord High First Secretary and Deputy Prime Minister.

"2. That he shall be regarded as the most important person in the Cabinet.

"3. That he will be in charge of all Cabinet committees to decide the government's policy on all matters.

"4. That in return for not being prime minister, he will be allowed to run the country.

"Signed and witnessed by Tarzan, Lord of the Jungle, Grand Big Beast and All-Powerful One. His mark."

I said to Mr Heseltine that I had drawn a line under anything I might have written before my unprecedented personal victory, and that therefore his piece of paper was not worth the paper it was written on. We then had an interesting conversation for two hours, and I eventually showed how in charge I was by agreeing to everything he wanted.

Friday

Mr Heseltine is taking his new job very seriously. He has already drawn up a list of who is to be in my new bastard-free Cabinet. I agree with all his suggestions, which are very sensible and should give my government an entirely fresh look so that we can beat Mr Blair. For instance, Mr Clarke will be Chancellor, Mr Howard will be the Home Secretary, Mr Gummer will be at the Environment ministry and instead of Mr Hurd, there will be Mr Rifkind, who has exactly the right deep voice for explaining that it would not be helpful to have a policy on the Single Currency yet. I shall be in no small measure sad to lose some old faces, such as Mr Hanley who has made such a tremendous contribution to putting across our policies to the country in the past two years. Also I have never known anyone so brilliant at solving crosswords since Mr Colthard who was in the mortgage department of the Standard Bank, where I worked in 1968. But there are several very exciting new faces to give my Cabinet a totally fresh look, e.g. Mr Freeman, Mr Hogg, and Mr Squitt who is only 23, and who will help us to win over the younger voters in time for the next election.

Saturday

This is the end of the most historic week since I became prime minister. For the first time I am my own man, except for the 109 MPs who didn't vote for me. One thing is certain; I show no animosity in my hour of total victory. I have always made it clear that Mr Redwood had a perfect right to stand against me, but now he must pay the price. I was very pleased to see that he now has to walk to work and open his own letters. Not that he will get any, except rude ones telling him what a bastard he is.

Also, I have won a tremendous victory against the press. They all said that if I was re-elected it would be a complete disaster for Britain. But they have all been proved totally wrong. I have been re-elected and the boil is totally lanced. This should shut them up for once and for all. As I said, "Put up or shut up." I put up, and they should shut up. That has been the verdict of the country. Oh yes.

Sunday

All the papers are attacking me again, saying that I have done a deal with Mr Heseltine and that I am no longer in full control. Mr Heseltine was also in no small measure annoyed and he rang to tell me to issue a denial of all the stories .

Later a big removal van drew up outside my house in Downing Street. "Go away," I said. "I am still the Prime Minister. Oh yes. The men laughed and began to unload a very large desk, a big swivel chair, and some exercise equipment, weights, etc.

"These are far too big for my office," I said in my special I-have-won voice. "No, not you, mate," said the man. "These are for Tarzan."

Monday

When I went to my office this morning I noticed that the wall where my *Daily Telegraph* World Map used to be has been turned into a very large door with two lights above it. One is red, saying "Wait" and the other is green, saying "Enter". I was just going to sit down when the green light went on, and the doors slid open. Imagine my not inconsiderable surprise when I saw on the other side a huge room the size of a football pitch, and at the far end an enormous desk with my friend Mr Heseltine sitting behind it. "Do come in, John," he shouted, "I'll be with you in a minute. I've just got a few important calls to make."

While I sat there I read the notice on his desk which said "Rt. Hon. M. Heseltine, Deputy Prime Minister, First Lord of the Jungle, Chairman of all Cabinet Committees, Primus Inter Pares and De-Facto Supreme Ruler of the Universe". I was just going to ask him what "Primus Inter Pares" meant, when Mr Heseltine finished his telephone call to Mr Herr Kohl and said: "Ah, John, I've got some good news for you. All this election business must

79

have been pretty tiring for you. You deserve a good long break, so I've decided to send you on holiday." I thought how lucky I am to have a deputy who is so considerate and thoughtful.

We were interrupted by a gang of workmen carrying a very big statue of Lord Nelson. "It looks just like the one in Trafalgar Square," I said. "It is the very same," said Mr Heseltine. "It has been lent to me by a grateful nation. Now if you'll excuse me, I have to ring Mr Yeltsin to see if he's dead yet."

Tuesday

I was just puzzling over the main headline in the *Telegraph*, "HEZZA RINGS YEZZA", when the new Party Chairman Mr Mawhinney came through my office. "Don't touch those papers, John," he shouted in his funny Irish voice. "I've put them out for Mr Heseltine. He wants to look at them before the Cabinet meeting he's called." "Oh," I said. "is there a Cabinet meeting?" "Not for you, John," he said. "You're officially on holiday." He then put a card into the sliding doors, and they opened. I was about to follow him when the doors shut again, and the red light went on saying "Wait". There is something very odd going on here, which I do not completely understand.

Wednesday

Today I have launched a great initiative which will win us the next election. It is perhaps my best idea to date, apart from my other great election-winning initiatives, which have been:

1. The Citizen's Charter

2. The Cones Hotline

3. Challenging myself for Leader of the Conservative Party and winning.

That is a record which any prime minister could be proud of. Oh yes.

My new idea is to have compulsory sport

in all schools, to help
us win back the
Ashes and have a
British champion at
Wimbledon.

I announced this
at a very important
press conference with
lots of famous
sporting personalities
such as Sir Stanley
Matthews, Rachel
Heyhoe-Flint and my
friend Jeffrey Archer,
the Olympic sprinter.
I explained my idea,
which was to spend
millions of pounds from the National Lottery on Olympic-
sized cricket pitches and tennis courts in all inner-city
playgrounds, so that every British child will have the chance
to win a gold medal for Britain. One very rude journalist
asked: "How can the children do sport when Mrs Shepherd
has sent them all off to get work experience in the factories?"
"Don't be silly!" I said, quick as a flash. "There aren't any
factories any more." Everyone laughed at this clever reply
and I was then photographed hitting a rugby ball at some
cricket stumps with a tennis racquet. Oh yes, it was a great
success.

Thursday

I had a not inconsiderably unpleasant nightmare last
night, from which I woke up screaming. Norma had to got to
the bathroom to get me a glass of Eno's Fruit Salts to calm
me down. I told her I had dreamed that I was sitting in my
office in the jungle when Mr Heseltine in a leopard-skin
swooped down on a creeper shouting: "Me Tarzan, you John.
Get me a banana at once!"

Fortunately when I got up in the morning I found that
everything was back to normal. Mr Heseltine was in a
meeting with the rest of the Cabinet and the red light was on.

As I sat there re-arranging my biros, including my special
"campaign pen" with the snappy slogan "Vote For Me And
Not Mr Redwood", Mr Hurd rang. "Hullo, prime minister," he
said. "I'm glad to see you're sticking to my Bosnia policy."
"What's that?" I said. "I thought we didn't have a Bosnia

policy?"

Mr Hurd laughed politely in his funny Old Etonian way. "Exactly, prime minister. I've just heard on the news that Mr Rifkind has called a special summit conference so that we can ask the Americans and all the others what to do."

This is a very good idea by Mr Rifkind and shows that Mr Hurd will not be missed.

"You see," I told Mr Hurd. "No one is indispensable." "How very true," said Mr Hurd and rang off. Mr Waldegrave then came in carrying a very big tray with a silver teapot and one huge mug marked "The Boss".

"That is very kind of you," I was just about to say, when the green light went on and Mr Waldegrave disappeared through the doors.

August

Friday

At last things are coming right, after my great election victory over Mr Redwood. There was a by-election in a place called Littleborough and Saddleworth, or was it Saddleborough and Littleworth? I must ask our new party chairman Mr Mawhinney. Anyway, all the newspapers said we were going to do very badly but we did not, as these results show;

Mervyn Cannabis-Smyth (Lib Dem)	14,612
Robin Dirtytricks (New Labour)	14,611
Sutch, Screaming Lord (Monster Raving Loony Party)	672
Blobby, Mr (Crinkley Bottom More Cash For Noelie Party)	671
The Hon. David Twistleton-Cholmondley-Spartlesworth (Dave Spart — Workers Revolutionary Front Against Veal Exports and the Criminal Justice Bill)	86

When you think how many people said we would get no
votes at all, it is obvious that we have pulled off a very
remarkable and encouraging result. The fight back has
begun. Oh yes.

Saturday

Today is a very unhistoric day and perhaps the blackest
day of my whole time as prime minister. Sir George Young,
who Mr Heseltine has put in charge of our Ministry of Traffic,
came in this morning to tell me the terrible news. Apparently
the Cones Hotline has been closed down. I asked Mr Sir
George Young if this was due to the very hot weather we have
been having recently. "No," he said, "it's just a pathetic idea
— whoever thought it up must have been a prize idiot."
"I think that might be a little harsh," I was beginning to tell
him, but he interrupted me in a manner which I consider in
my judgement to be rather rude. "Listen," he said. "It has cost
the taxpayer £815,000 a day. Only three people have rung up
since last July. And they were wrong numbers." I made a note
to tell Mr Heseltine when I get back from holiday that he has
made in my view a very poor appointment. It is quite obvious
that Mr Sir George Young has no idea how important cones
are, and that the Cones Hotline could have won us the next
election. If we lose, we shall all know who to blame!

Sunday

At last I am in the heart of Europe, which is where I
always said I would be. You see, another election promise
kept! Today my wife Norman and I arrived for our holiday at
a little village called Prozac in a place called Dordogne which
is in France. It is very nice and everyone is very friendly. My
first job was to fix the filter on the swimming pool, and I
decided to ask the French peasant next door to assist since all
the instructions were written in German. I could not help
noticing that he was reading the *Daily Telegraph*.
Nevertheless I decided that it would only be polite to speak to
him in his own language. "Excusez-moi, monsieur," I said.
"Ou-est la gare, s'il vous plait?". He looked at me in surprise
and said in perfect English: "I know who you are. You're that
Terry Major-Ball who's always on the telly. My wife's a big

fan. In fact we've brought your book out to read by the pool. I've just got to the bit where your brother paints all the gnomes with the wrong colour hats. Fiona and I nearly died laughing." I decided that we could do without the swimming pool filter after all.

Monday

It is very like Britain here in Europe, which proves just how those Euro-sceptics have got it all wrong. The French have copied many things from the English way of life. On our way to the village shop, which is called Le Tesco, we even saw a cricket match being played. When one old French peasant took a wicket, another shouted out, "I say, Nigel, jolly well bowled." It is amazing how like us they are. Mr Portaloo and Mr Redwood would soon change their tune if they came here. Perhaps Mr Heseltine could organise a holiday for them here too. This evening Norman and I went out to a typical local restaurant, since we had been told that Dordogne is famous for its French cuisine. It was called "The Frog and Trumpet" and served such traditional dishes as "Le Ploughman's", "Le Scampi et Frites" and "Le Pizza — Pan Profond". It was very delicious indeed. I am now totally relaxed and have completely stopped thinking about Mr Blair and his so-called New Labour Party, which is not new at all in my judgement.

Tuesday

I was just beginning to wonder what was happening back in England, when we bumped into our other neighbour, Monsieur Fishwick, putting out his empty gas cylinder. "I see good old Hezza's getting the country sorted out at last while that idiot Major's abroad," he said. "All in the *Express*," he went on. "Do you want to borrow it?" I took his paper back to our gîte to read by the pool and saw that Mr Heseltine had called a huge press conference

to announce his plans for the country. "I am going to abolish the Civil Service, burn all the red tape and save Britain £300 billion," he had said. "There are too many grey men in positions of power who should be sacked, or at least sent off on long holidays." For some reason I am beginning to be suspicious of Mr Heseltine. I read this out to Norman who said: "You should watch your back, John." "That is very kind of you, Norman," I said. "Will you please rub in some more of that sun cream?"

Wednesday

Today my wife Norman and I went to see the historic cave paintings at Mogadon. It was very dark inside and to my mind the paintings looked like doodles of the type that Mr Waldegrave does on his pad during cabinet meetings. I did not like them. Oh no.

On the coach on the way back I sat next to Monsieur Newman. He spoke perfect English too and said he had heard something amazing on the World Service. Apparently Mr Heseltine had scored a great triumph in getting a German firm called Siemens to set up in Britain.

"Hezza's the only one with any flair," agreed a Madame Cash, who has a big house nearby. "That's right," struck up Madame Atullah who apparently owns a lot of the land where we are staying. "He's the Prime Minister in all but name."

Then the whole coach joined in a rousing chorus of "Oh My Darling Heseltine" all the way home.

Monday

My wife Norman and I are still on our holiday in France. We are definitely relaxing and not thinking about any of the following at all:

Mr Heseltine.
Mr Blair.
Mr Redwood.
My brother Terry.
Mrs Thatcher.
All the other Bastards.

Oh no.

Today we are at a very nice place called Nice. You see, the French use English words for their towns, which shows how wrong the Euro-sceptics are about them. They have even called this part of France the Riviera, after the famous Cornish Riviera, and the main street is called the Promenade of the English, which shows just how at the heart of Europe we are and always have been. Oh yes.

Tuesday

Today my office in London rang me to say that they were faxing me a very historic letter which had arrived from Mr Phuwotascorcha, who is this week's prime minister of Japan. I went down to the hotel fax machine, which is next to the swimming pool, to receive this very important document in person.

Unfortunately it was being read by a large German man who was laughing out loud and showing it to his wife. I was not inconsiderably annoyed as this particular couple had already taken my sun-lounger earlier in the day. When I finally got the fax back, this is what it said:

Honourable Prime Minister,

We would like to salute you on your historic victory over despicable traitor John Ledwood. May we take this opportunity also to convey our deepest condolences over your country's recent failure to win the cricket match over the West Indies. We in Japan know what it is like to be cheated of much-deserved victory at the last minute owing to circumstances beyond our control. Geddit?

Your infinitely humble and obedient superior,

N. PHUWOTASCORCHA

There was a little note with this letter from Mr Rifkind which said:

"Great news, John. This is the nearest to a full apology for the war we're ever going to get. You've pulled off a real triumph here. Better than anything Mrs Thatcher ever did. Michael says you should stay on holiday a couple of weeks longer to celebrate. He will hold the fort."

Wednesday

I do not know whether to be not inconsiderably annoyed or

not inconsiderably pleased. This morning I saw on the hotel's CNN News that no sooner have I turned my back then the great economic recovery has come to an end. This only goes to show how wrong I was to leave Mr Heseltine in charge. According to Ted Bruback and Barbara Freephone, the presenters of CNN's *Good Morning Globe* show, there has been a rise in Britain's unemployment.

"That is only because you sacked Mr Redwood, Mr Hanley and those others," said my wife Norman. For once she may have got it right. This small increase is only a temporary blip caused by seasonal factors — i.e. my reshuffle and Mr Gummer's drought — and everything will soon be back to normal.

Thursday

I am extremely pleased with my new Chairman of the Party, Mr Mawhinney. I have at last managed to find a copy of last week's *Daily Telegraph* to read about the test score, and I was delighted to see on the front page, next to a picture of Miss Hurley, that Mr Mawhinney has really got Mr Blair on the ropes. Instead of just sitting around doing the crossword like Mr Hanley, he has discovered a Labour council somewhere in the North of England who have wasted huge amounts of taxpayers' money erecting a statue of a hippopotamus. This is the kind of thing which will win us the next election. Oh yes. I am sure that in the months to come Mr Mawhinney will find more statues in other towns, perhaps of other animals.

Friday

This morning I set my alarm clock for 4.30 a.m. to be sure of getting to the sunlounger before our fat German friend. Norman was not amused. "Why are you suddenly so keen to beat the Germans?" she snapped. "Normally you do whatever they say." Unfortunately when I got to the pool I found that Mr Herr

Wurst-Thurn was already there. "Ach, guten morgen, Herr
Major," he said, with a smile. "So, ze early bird fails to catch
ze worm." I was in no small measure annoyed and went back
to my room to watch the CNN Early Morning News with Phil
and Janine. They said that the Japanese prime minister's
letter to me had not been meant to be an apology at all, but
only a letter to Mr Heseltine congratulating him on becoming
prime minister.

Sunday

I decided that today would be a very historic day when I
would finally outwit Herr Wurst-Thurn by getting to the sun-
lounger at 1 o'clock in the morning. Imagine my surprise
when I discovered my German friend already on the lounger,
reading a very fat book called *Der Jeffrey Archer Omnibus bei
der Englischer Meistergeschicktespieler J. Archole, Schreiber
von Keine Ein Pfennig Mehr, Zwolf Rote Heringen und alte
meisterwerke*. Once again I was forced to return to my room
to watch Bill and Jodie presenting Midnight News Plus, Live
From Atlanta. They said that the Japanese prime minister
had apologised again, properly this time. They also said that:
"British premier Heseltine had welcomed the apology and
thanked the Japanese people for their courage, honesty and
car factories."

DEAR BILL

An occasional series of letters from
Denis Thatcher to his old golfing partner
Bill Deedes. Found in No. 10 Downing
Street and marked
'Intercepted and Forwarded by MI5'.

OCTOBER 1994

Dear Bill,

What price the bullfighter joke overleaf? My Portuguese is a bit rusty, but I take it to be some reference to singing treble in the choir. I thought he had a look of Portillo about him, it may be the lipstick.

God, do I not like to be beside the seaside!

Re your enquiry about the Boss's health. I read in one of the blatts — I think the one where they'd covered her face in whitewash — that due to painful dentistry she had been forced to subsist for the last six months on a diet of soup. Electric soup would be nearer the truth. You or I, Bill, would put it down to hitting the bottle about as hard as it is possible to hit it, even by Maurice's standards. Ever since she got the Julius Caesar treatment from Geoffrius Mogodonus and his fellow Conspirators the old girl has been swilling them down as if there was no tomorrow, which, given the list of charges pending for the Boy Mark, it seems quite likely there won't be (at least for Swiss Family Thatcher).

What the buggers in the press don't seem to understand is that every penny of the Sheikh's £12 million bung has already been earmarked by the grasping Burgerdorff harpie and her lawyers for "aggravated psychological cruelty". Where Margaret is going to find another arms contract to pay for the rest of the trial, I have no idea.

The widow's gong is sounding and tiffin calls.

Yours on remand,

DENIS

DECEMBER 1994

Dear Bill,

Did you see that M. has been in trouble over arms again? Not, this time, I am glad to say, the Boy Mark, still recovering in hospital from his mother's visit in a marriage guidance capacity, but a slimy little fellow from the College of Heralds who arrived at Chester Square with a real dog's breakfast of a design showing some bearded Bertie in woolly jumper shoring up Margaret's crest in company with a blindfolded woman in a nightdress selling something out of a pair of scales. I can't remember what the motto was, but it was something to do with keeping your end up and being one of us.

What was particularly annoying was that I had just that same evening with the help of my little friend Baggers, an artistic johnny who sometimes earns a bob or two helping behind the bar at the RAC, roughed out what seemed to me an infinitely superior version.

The shield part, Baggers and I decided, should have one of those sharp points that you poke people in the eye with, and then in the little square bits a Dead Argie couchant hoist on a torpedo gules — this is the lingo these fellows use, as I discovered when they did mine — then on the other side Margaret mounted on a dragon slaying Arthur Scargill. The bottom half was then divided into two, with a Sheikh rampant handing over a sack of readies on one side, and on the other the BT prancing fairy escaping from the serpent coils of Nationalisation.

Supporting the crest, where this woolly-jersied buffoon now stands, was myself, G&T in hand and smiling serenely in my Inverness cape, golf bag over one shoulder. On the other our generous patron Rupert M. making generous advances to my little woman in the form of a very large cheque. Above were crossed handbags, and below the motto "We Are A Grandmother", which would obviously have to be put into Latin.

I was going to ask Waldegrave, but he warned me that translating work of that kind came very expensive, so I left it until I next run into Enoch P.

Unfortunately, when I showed this to Garter Pursuivant Extraordinary (E.F. Ratner-Leng — you probably remember him from Huntercombe) he was very snooty and said these things had to be done by trained heralds. The identical design also happened to belong to Lord Montagu who would certainly sue for breach of copyright if we pinched his motto.

Baggers, I can tell you, was pretty miffed when I broke the news to him, as he had put a lot of work into it, and had had to spend a whole afternoon in the Library to get the Argie uniform right. I enclose his drawing. Maybe your local Conservative Association could use it for their Christmas Card. I know they're none too keen on the present incumbent.

I wish I could tell you better news of the old girl's mental health, but alas I cannot. Last week I caught her on the roof at Chester Square tossing tiles into the street and saying she wasn't coming down till we got out of Europe.

Yours in injury time,

DENIS

**CHESTER SQUARE
SW1**

APRIL 1995

Dear Bill,

Thank you for your v. sympathetic p.c. re M. in the *Daily Telegraph* photograph where the old girl was being held up by two security men. I agree that she was not looking her best, but a bottle and a half of scotch before breakfast, as you and I well know, can weaken the knees even of the strongest. M., as you know, has always liked a snort but more so of late. Personally I blame Major for letting things slip. She certainly does. The other night sitting in her chair, having screamed a good deal, she launched into an uncharacteristically lurid attack on him, claiming that he had never been "one of us" and she must have been "temporarily insane" to entrust him with her life's achievement of eradicating socialism from these islands.

There has also been, I will admit, the contributing factor of the Boy Mark. Some malodorous and red-nosed New Zealander called Hallowheen has been through the press cuttings and produced a book about him in collaboration with someone who knows how to spell. Knowing my distaste for the subject, you will understand the eager anticipation with which I opened it, hoping at last for a stake that could be driven through the vampire's heart. But, alas, the Maori piss-artist had only managed to discover one new scrap of tattle i.e. that the wretched son and h. had arrived in the Middle East with a signed chitty from the boss saying that, unlikely as it might seem, the bearer was her son and she hoped that people would make allowances for him ideally to the tune of several million petrodollars.

Margaret, needless to say, treated this pathetic bundle of old rope as a cue for fresh lamentations, wailing in the small hours and beating her head against the cocktail cabinet. "My poor innocent son! I know what it is like to be slandered by these inhuman thugs. Now they are suggesting that he has had his hand in my foundation and has been disowned by his father-in-law Mr Burgerdorf. This is the fall of the House of Thatcher. We shall not see its like again."

As if this were not enough, the doorbell rings well past midnight and the cause of all the trouble arrives on the doorstep heavily muffled, wearing a false beard against recognition by the encamped reptiles, and asking if we could lend him a few million to see him over the weekend. Fortunately M. was upstairs under sedation and I was able to take him into the wine cellar and give him a very large piece of what was left of my mind. Not that it will have the slightest effect. Having cursed me roundly — "pathetic hen-pecked old soak" to use his exact words — he flounced out into the night, saying he could raise the money in five minutes from Jeffrey Archer.

I wish this was the end of the story. Carol is in the throes of writing my biography — "Life With Father". She comes round with her notebook at all hours of the day and night trying to get me to remember at least one anecdote from the past. Mercifully, it is all a purple haze and she is having to make it all up with the help of a Mr Sherrin in Chelsea. Shall I see you in Portugal? The widow Flack is having the other hip done but that should not prevent her from ladling out the snorts.

Yours on the Zimmer,

DENIS

JUNE 1995

Dear Bill,

I'm glad to hear you enjoyed my eightieth. My own memories of it are somewhat hazy, at least after midnight. Did Maurice really abseil down through the skylight to do his SAS Gorillagram or did I imagine that? I woke up in the Intensive Care at Torquay, the nearest emergency facilities for geriatrics to Downing Street, and the chief medico, a very agreeable Ghanaian, told me I had the constitution of a man of a hundred. He said I was very lucky not to be conscious for so much of the time: if I had been compos mentis when I played that silly prank with the fire extinguisher I would almost certainly be in prison.

I don't know whether you remember that story we used to have to read at school about the man who lived his life backwards? Dickens? Jeffrey Archer? No matter. Much the same thing is happening to poor Margaret. After hitting the jackpot with her first volume of old rope, she was persuaded to get her ghost train of dons, hacks, toadies, etc, led by the impressively inebriate Professor Stone of Oxford, to recall for her her early years at Grantham.

This produced weeks of schoolgirlish giggling from the winos in the writing pool, but the results failed to impress little Mr Fishwick from Collins, who said it needed spicing up. Dr Stone pencilled in a few steamy scenes in the Quad at Somerville featuring Dame Daphne Park and the late Edith Summerskill, but this was immediately blue-pencilled by the former Fuhrer on the grounds that it might upset Lord Blake.

In the end they settled for a no-holds-barred butt in the stomach for little Major, details to be leaked to the *Sunday Times* to coincide with the re-publication launch.

Stone accordingly tottered in with is tape-recorder and asked the Boss how she viewed recent developments. I new this was a mistake and within moments I was upstairs rooting through the medicine chest for her box of Prozac. When I got back the little needle on Dr Branestawm's recorder was banging about in the red bit of the dial and the academic himself was reaching down into his briefcase for another bottle of electric soup.

"That pathetic little man. All thrown away. Stabbed in the back at the moment of victory! See him toadying to that awful German, giving away our ancient liberties to the Hun!" Stone's bloodshot orbs focused for a moment, and he leaned forward to interrupt her. "Prime Minister, might you consider a return if the nation called in its hour of need?"

"No, Norman, no." she replied, wiping her lips with the tablecloth as the Prozac began to do its deadly work. "My day is done. It will be for others to take up the sword from where I left it in the stone. Der Tag! Der Tag!" At this her eyelids flickered and she lost consciousness.

When this had been suitably edited, a draft was submitted to Friend Fishwick, who rubbed his hands, said he was sure Mr Murdoch would be delighted, and ordered another two hundred thousand copies to be printed on the strength of it.

It was the next morning at breakfast, when she had a chance to read the press release, that she asked to speak to Dr Stone on the telephone. "Norman? Why did you let me say this? I must have been mad. Of course there's no question of throwing in the towel yet! Look at de Gaulle, look at Mitterrand! He carried on while they were measuring him for his coffin. Portillo is too young, Redwood is a fool. Lamont perhaps, but not yet. No, Norman, I shall be ready. Let the people know they have only to sound the trumpet and I shall emerge from my cave like Arthur of yore, the Once and Future Leader! Denis, go and open another bottle of my medicine. No buts, you will not be there to see me..."

Her latest wheeze to annoy Major is to lavish praise on Brother Blair, which will also annoy the smelly-socks no end.

Shall I see you at Huntercombe for Old Oystereyes' VJ Day Fancy Dress Match?

Yours Octogenerically,

DENIS

ALSO AVAILABLE FROM
PRIVATE EYE • CORGI

MAGIC EYE
*A New Way of
Looking at the World*

THE BEST OF
PRIVATE EYE 1995
£ 4.99

THE PRIVATE EYE BOOK OF
CRAIG BROWN PARODIES

*In this brand new collection of
parodies, Craig Brown extends
a welcoming claw to Margaret
Thatcher, Newman and
Baddiel, Martin Amis, Linda
McCartney and Michael
Winner, among many others.*
£ 4.99

SON OF YOBS
*Another collection of Yobs
and other cartoons by Tony
Husband in this sequel to
the best-selling 'YOBS'.*
£ 3.99